THE LIGHT OF EXPERIENCE

THE LIGHT
OF EXPERIENCE

BRITISH BROADCASTING CORPORATION

PUBLISHED BY THE
BRITISH BROADCASTING CORPORATION
35 MARYLEBONE HIGH STREET
LONDON WIM 4AA

ISBN 0 563 17430 7

FIRST PUBLISHED 1977

PRINTED IN ENGLAND BY
TONBRIDGE PRINTERS LTD
PEACH HALL WORKS, SHIPBOURNE ROAD
TONBRIDGE, KENT

CONTENTS

T*he Light of Experience* is about first-hand, personal experience. One person talks straight to camera about some personal crisis or watershed and why it has such significance for them. The territory we explore is the inner. There is no end to the richness of the inner life, no country so varied, no journey so eventful; and in following these stories we realise the quality, the strength, the resilience that lies in people, even if we don't always see it.

The success of the programmes has been something of a surprise to those who work on them. It is, after all, a short and simple programme. In television terms it has a very small budget and it is not shown at a peak viewing time. Yet the response from viewers is unarguable – it seems to speak to a wide range of people at a level of shared humanity.

I think the reason for this lies in the authority of experience. It is the one thing you can trust – and when someone is talking from their own experience, then you must believe them. This has always been so, from early man discovering a taste for meat, to St Paul's conversion on the Damascus Road and the strange power of reason-defying love. Every time we admit to an unexplained pain, an invisible emotion, feelings of fear, wonder or joy for which there is no external evidence, we are saying something which cannot be denied. If I say I am hungry it makes no difference if you tell me I ate an hour ago – I'm still hungry!

Truth can be understood at many levels and there have been times when reason has reigned supreme and experience has been seen as deceptive. The balance continually changes. But the 1970s are a time when institutions are suspect, dogma unpopular and doubt is round every corner. Our own experience is all that is left to us that cannot be questioned. And even if it is, we can defend it to the last breath because we know it to be true.

So much for theory. In practice one of the pleasures of making these programmes has been the opportunity to meet people at this level of their personal experience. Those who have contributed deserve many tributes. Gratitude especially for the patience they've shown in tackling the technical demands of television – often a strange new world – for the work they have put into the scripts and for so much cooperation in finding visual material, from raiding family albums to lending treasured objects. But most of all I have valued the fact that they have been prepared to share their most precious possession – their own experience.

SHIRLEY DU BOULAY
Series Producer

Production Team
MALCOLM STEWART
JOHN WILCOX
INGRID DUFFELL
STEPHANIE MITCHELL

ARCHIE HILL

CLOSED WORLD OF LOVE

I wasted the first thirty years of my life. Those years took me into many personal dark corners where I existed inside a vacuum. I seemed always to be on the outside of life, looking in at things to envy. I think I was more of a wound than a person.

When I was a young man I travelled a hard road as a drunk, lived rough for longer than I care to remember and sat in the stagnancy of prison cells and alcoholic institutions.

I was the eldest but one of eleven children brought up in the lean days of the pre-war Depression, and you don't go down on your knees in *that* sort of environment and thank God for his blessings. You are too intent making sure you have got a place in the street-corner free-soup-queue, too busy surviving to worry about the hereafter. God didn't seem to be sharing my life and I wasn't much concerned with him. It's only very recently that I did accept God as being real as the churches would have me believe and I was filled with loathing, hatred and contempt for this God. I wanted to meet him face to face, to spit on Him, to throttle Him slowly with my own two hands. I wanted God to be real, so that I could do that to Him. My hatred for Him was the most intense experience of my life, including six years with the armed forces, including time spent as a homeless drop-out and a convict. It came about because of my twenty-six-year-old stepson, born to my wife's first marriage. He is a hundred per cent physically and mentally handicapped; a number wiped off God's blackboard.

Barry can't walk, talk, feed or toilet himself, or do any solitary thing. He is twenty-six years old and still my wife has to wash him, just like a baby. Sometimes his eyes are bright with know-ledge but his body gets weaker and weaker and more and more useless. I marvelled that such a body could have kept the flame of life burning for so long. Every morning we go through the slow ritual of undressing Barry. This is a task he resents strangers doing for him, but when my wife and I do it his eyes tell us that he trusts us. Perhaps he feels the affection in our hands.

I estimate that my wife has changed 35,000 nappies in his life-time. For twenty years, she had to wash those nappies after use: it's only recently that she learnt that disposable nappies were available. Happiness for my wife became a disposable nappy. We have to cut slits into Barry's shoes so my wife can make sure his toes aren't doubled over. If they are it's painful. He will be in pain all day and he won't be able to tell us. He is not heavy to lift – he only weighs five stone – but it is difficult to manage him. Some-times his limbs convulse and you could drop him. Death is not necessarily the worst thing that can happen provided it is peace-ful, but we are frightened of making his existing disabilities worse. Four or five times a day he has to be fed. My wife must have spoon-fed 37,000–47,000 meals into his mouth. Sometimes each meal takes an hour because he has difficulty in swallowing. This means trips back to the kitchen to reheat the food.

There is a great bond of life between mother and son, and a deep closed world of love; and I love him too, as if he were my own flesh and blood. Recently he was operated on to have a lump removed from his groin, and it turned out to be cancer. So now we take each day at a time and wait for him to die. When I learned of the cancer I felt that Christ's words 'Suffer little chil-dren to come unto me' weren't true: the words were 'Let little children suffer', as Barry has suffered for so many long droning years. I couldn't see any 'God's purpose' in what was happening to Barry and my wife, only God's spite and malice. If there is a God, then when He made my wife's son His hands trembled with some dark malice. He was in an angry, indifferent mood, filled with private petulance. But my wife believes in God. 'God will love him,' she says. And I am angry that she thinks this, because this God she believes in is the ugliness which rejected him in the first place, and gave her a geriatric treadmill to walk for more than twenty-six years.

My wife and I had watched a television programme about thalidomide children and my wife said: 'I wish Barry had been born thalidomide, it would be a ninety per cent improvement upon what he is'. And her quiet remark hit me between the eyes and stunned my brain, so that I could have sat down and wept blood. For twenty-six years to be locked inside a useless prison of flesh; no external signs to indicate whether the computor of his mind is fully at work. And I hope it isn't. Because if it is, if it has been, then he has been a castaway isolated in a tiny strip of land poking up from a dark deep sea, deep and dreadful, and lonely. I hope he has a quick and not a lingering death to wipe him clean, to blow his candle-flame out.

And how can we tell our young son Robin that his brother is dying? His mouth will droop to sadness because he won't understand, because I don't understand. I shall dredge up empty clichés, comforting homilies. I shall give him verse and text and chapter. But the poison which is filling me must not infect him. When we first came to live here and my young son started school he seemed so alone and forlorn, so devoid of friends. And I wondered about it, and felt sad because of it, perhaps because it reminded me of my own lonely boyhood. I think I found the answer for the loneliness in his brother Barry, who spends so much time sitting in his wheelchair, watching the world go by. Kids passing to and from school could see him there, and I heard one of them say to another that Barry was 'a dummy'. And I knew then that that was why Robin wasn't making friends, that our crippled boy was the barrier between him and other boys of his age.

I wondered if I should keep Barry out of sight as the children passed by – and then thought: 'If I do that, why not go the whole hog and put Barry in the cellar and chain him to the wall, and give him straw to sleep on?' I went to my young son's school and showed slides to the children of handicapped people who were cut off from social life. Not violent or unpleasant pictures, but 'pretty' pictures. And I explained to the kids what being handicapped was and asked them what they could do if they had someone in their street who was handicapped. 'Please sir,' they said, 'we could knock on the door and ask the lady of the house if we could run errands for her'. 'Please sir, we could ask to take the cripple out in his wheelchair for a walk'. Anyway, it worked. Robin's got many friends now, and brings his special pals home for meals, or even to stay weekends with him. They accept Barry for what he is, a human being who got short-changed by fate. But the period was a difficult one. Robin could have grown up to resent his brother, be ashamed of him. Equally, my wife and I could have foisted responsibilities onto him like 'Barry-sitting' and things like that. But from the very start, when Robin was born, we knew that Barry was our responsibility and not Robin's. What Robin does for Barry he does unselfishly, not from a sense of duty. He makes things to try and keep him entertained, toys, battery-worked lightbulbs which flash on and off and he enjoys it.

My wife plans the planting of the garden each year so that she can take Barry around when the flowers are in bloom. She plants them so that they are the right height for him to see from his chair. Does he take it in? Can he appreciate it? I don't know, but it's an attempt to stimulate his mind, to involve him as far as we can in the normalities of life and nature. The very normalities which life and nature have denied him.

Some time ago I stood behind Barry's wheelchair in the garden and tried to see what he could see. I mentally locked my feet against the floor so that I was helplessly fixed in a single position; dependent upon someone's charity or love to move me. What I could see was a small enough world. His wasted neck-muscles gave him no more than thirty-degrees of head-turn; they narrowed his frontal vision to almost straight ahead. He could see people and events pass in front of his eyes, but could not turn his head to follow them to some sort of conclusion. Housewives with shopping bags passed up and down the street. He knew many of them by sight, through long hours at the window, and gurgled greetings to them which they couldn't hear. As I stood there I willed one or two to look up our pathway to the window where he sat, to smile for him and wave a greeting. But passers-by were too absorbed in their own problems to see a boy at a window. They were just brush-strokes upon the small canvas of Barry's frontal vision. Each stroke separate with no plan or purpose or relationship.

'Put Barry away' the doctor told my wife when he was eleven months old. 'He will never walk or talk or do anything for himself. Put him away and forget about him, and have another'. And I remembered when I was a boy in a farmyard near my home and the sow had farrowed and given out more piglets than she'd got dugs to feed from, and the weak chap of the litter grew weaker and weaker. A runt from birth, a loser and his siblings pushed him to one side as he and they squealed for the milk-dugs. 'He winna mek it, gaffer', the pigman said to the farmer, and the farmer shrugged like God. 'Put it down, then', he said, 'and let the sow get on with it'. And I saw the pigman take the piglet by its hind-legs, its squealing and pleading to be allowed to live, and he dashed its head against a wall. And the piglet died whilst its community of brothers and sisters gurgled and grunted at the pleasurable udders. 'Put him away', the doctors said. To her, his mother, my wife. They did not look at her when they said it, they looked away. Because if they had looked at her they would have seen God-hope in her eyes; and they knew that God was gone away. She did not 'put him away'. She took him away – she took him away to her secret places of motherhood and womanhood. She took him away and kept him, and in the keeping relinquished most of her own life. She gave her own life as an extension of her son's.

I suppose, when she took him home and did not 'put him away' as the doctors advised her to – I suppose she hoped they were wrong. He was such a beautiful baby, clean-limbed and perfectly formed. He was a dark-haired baby with brown eyes that laughed out at the world. She doted upon a miniature of perfection which would soon show the development of gross imperfection, the decay in the bud. I don't think, then, that she thought her son would be imprisoned in a wheelchair all of his life, and she a prisoner with him never able to develop her own creativities. But in her mind she wasn't tied by fetters of duty but by love. A closed world of love. So rich a world, it is beyond description. I'd never met love like this before – my ideas of love had been so shallow. What privileged few amongst us really do know what love is? We know self-love, pride-love, power-love, comfort-love, dependent-love. We know shallow-love and glitter-love, and love by many other names; we know man-woman love which, as time passes and youth with it, turns into safe and comfortable habit. There are good and rich loves, most of them; but there are different levels of love and the deepest depth of all is this closed world of love between a mother and a useless creature which was the child drawn in pain from her body into a poisoned light of day.

A sixteen-year age-gap exists between Barry and Robin. But in every respect of development except actual age, Robin is now older than Barry. But Barry was firmly established in his needs and dependence when Robin was born and perhaps my wife didn't want Robin to be born. Partly, perhaps in secret fear that he, like Barry, might be born imperfect, and partly because she knew that Barry was a full-time responsibility. But equally she was sad for me, knowing a man's proudness in a son to fulfil the dreams, perhaps, that he himself has not achieved. When she conceived my young son I tortured myself with guilt because of the conception. Could she cope with the dual role of responsibility, had she enough of herself to share? Would after all a twisted-ugly fate duplicate the errors of Barry in the new life to come? The fates were kind, they gave no abnormality.

Perhaps I love Robin more than I love Barry, I don't know. I don't think so. But Robin is a boy who runs to me, happy in the coming, joyful in the union of dad and son. Barry I have to go to, lean over, make comfortable, help care for his body-needs. Constantly, I am aware that I must often be his arms and legs. I can enter into Robin's life and share it, but cannot enter into Barry's.

I can only guess what goes on inside his mind. I wonder if he is lonely and cut off in there. Sometimes in his eyes I see a deep dark aliveness staring out at me, an equal intelligence, and I find myself almost expecting him to speak.

One night I wrapped him in a blanket and took him onto the back porch and let him look at the sky. I had not thought to do this before. Suddenly I wanted to give him new experiences, to share with him some deepness from inside myself. I wanted to fill his mind with happy wonder. Things I had taken for granted, like moon and stars and night, suddenly seemed filled with magic. Sitting with him on the porch I felt some strange awe. An explanation of how I'd become me. How millions of microscopic sperm-seeds were sent on a long hard journey. How for a full-grown man to compete with this sperm-journey he would have to cross the Sahara on foot, swim ten miles upstream against a raging current, climb the Alps and walk half-way across Siberia. If one of the seeds had reached the egg instead of my seed, I would not have come into existance. And I looked at Barry and marvelled that the seed which became him had won through. And it came to me, suddenly, that the end of life – Barry's or mine – was not important. The miracle of everything came about with the seed's journey, which brought life into being. Sitting with Barry I looked at the stars and knew that we are both part of that same system.

I have learned rich things from Barry. Things I could never have learned from the Bible or pulpit, or churches. I think I will treasure always the trust and affection he had for me. I will remember, always, the way his eyes lit up as I walked towards him. He is deep of my soul, because he has added dimensions to it.

I asked my wife what I must do when Barry dies. 'A handful of family', she answered, 'And cremate him. I can't bear to think of him underground'. So open his prison and let him blow free and ride the wind until the ashes settle and maybe, next year, next Spring, he will nourish the flowers. I think of those years that I have wasted, and about people whom I have hurt and I measure this, myself, against Barry's twenty-six years of physically help-less existance, and know then that his life has been the purer life. Everything about him exudes gentleness. He has not known hate or malice, greed or spite, or self-pity. He has not known lusts or angers, or selfishness. He has not exploded his frustrations like shrapnel to inflict wounds against those around him.

Now, when selfishness or self-pity start to poison me, I think of wheelchaired Barry. And from his helplessness, I find a strength and tenacity of purpose filling me up. And then I do not seek to question 'God's will' but I put my trust in the sacred woman, Nature, and know that the feeling of heartbreak in the heart of things is but a moment's human hesitation on the thresh-old of a deep, serene, purposeful unknown. And thinking so, I almost touch that peace which surpasses understanding.

ROBERT VAN DE WEYER
AN UNEXPECTED GURU

I was a pupil at Westminster School in the shadow of the Houses of Parliament and the Abbey. A school for the children of wealth and privilege, born with silver spoons in our mouths. My own family made its money in merchant banking in the early years of the Industrial Revolution. The wealth inherited from that time paid my school fees, and in return I was imbued with the spirit and moral doctrine on which the Industrial Revolution was built – the doctrine of enlightened self-interest, pursuit of the highest gain, the belief that happiness equals income. When I entered public school, the sense of privilege was vanishing. By the time I had left it had almost gone. We were no longer set apart from the rest of our generation; we listened to the same music, watched the same television programmes, dreamed the same dreams. Luxury for almost everybody was pouring off the factory conveyor belts, and a whole generation, born since the war, was growing up with a silver spoon – smaller, perhaps, than ours at Westminster, but silver none the less. And London had begun to swing.

The pursuit of material pleasure had turned into a stampede by the early 1960s and with a 2d bus-ride from school I could be in the midst of it. After classes each day I would wander through the streets of Soho or into the great pagan temples of the West End department stores. I would observe the faces of the shoppers; middle-aged women, like tribal warriors on a treck for the best buy; young men nervously trying on a new battle-dress, the latest flared trousers or Afghan coats; girls out hunting the latest fashions and buying face-paint for their weekend rituals. Alone amongst these tribal hordes I had no money, so occasionally I would steal the things that took my fancy – a shirt, a record, a book.

During the late 1960s new attitudes and concerns were in the air, the records we were hearing, and the magazines we were reading, began to tell a new story, proclaiming the coming of psychedelia, the experiences to be found in LSD and cannabis. And we responded to the call. So while our parents were seeking happiness in the department store, we were taking the illusion one stage further into absurdity, seeking happiness in pills and brown lumps of hashish. But for many of us – myself included – the drug trip meant far more than this. When, for example, you smoke hashish you can often feel a sense of being lifted up; and if you surrender to this force rather as a young person surrenders in love, you do have a glimpse of an alternative, a fleeting glimmer of an interior, spiritual reality. I did experience this and it contrasted with the crude unreality of exterior life. One such unreality on a grand scale was, for many of us at that time, the Vietnam War.

So for us the late 1960s were the time of the Vietnam demonstrations. The sight of the richest nation in the world destroying thousands of innocent people confirmed what the drugs were already telling us. We would emerge bleary-eyed from a Saturday night trip, to protest outside the American Embassy on Sunday afternoon.

Though I thought myself a rebel I accepted my father's cash when I wanted it and early in 1969 when I had just left school my father offered me £300 on which to travel the world and I took it and set out for India for the first time. When I set out I had a vague notion that the drug experience was connected with religion, though I didn't know how. In the holy men of India, the gurus and the ascetics, I perceived in its fullness the interior reality which I had glimpsed through drugs. By the time I returned from India, nine months later, I was convinced that religion somehow held the key to human happiness.

The India which I got to know was the hot, dry, dusty plains; the villages built of mud and cow-dung; and the grubby little temples. I ate the peasant diet of unleaven bread and watery lentils and most of my travelling was on foot. In the city's bazaars I found that special Indian quality, a mixture of smells and sounds and the sights of ancient India blended with the modern age.

I spent a few months collecting gurus. Whenever I heard a local guru being highly recommended, I would prepare a list of questions, find an interpreter, and go and sit at his feet. Some treated my questions with contempt as the product of a literal western mind. But most welcomed me warmly, treated my simplicity and lack of understanding with kindness, and exuded a serenity and joy which took me by complete surprise. Often these gurus would tell me that I thought too much, that my soul was in my head, that true understanding comes only when the intellect surrenders. My hackles would always rise at this: to suspend one's critical faculties is the ultimate heresy of the western liberal education.

I would desperately needle them to define the words they used. For example, what is the soul and what did they mean by perfect knowledge? Their reaction would be amused disdain which used to annoy me. But one day in the town of Mysore I suddenly found myself making a decision to abandon the mental disciplines drummed into me during years of western schooling and to set off on foot in a remote part of central India, trying out myself the life of the wandering holy man, begging for food and shelter.

For three weeks I was alone, dependent entirely on the generosity of village people who spoke no English, walking through mile after mile of parched, brown countryside, in the hottest season of the year. At times I came close to madness. The aggression latent within me would suddenly rise up and explode at some villager who happened to nod at a greeting. For hours on end, as the hot sun clasped my head like a heavy chain, I would be obsessed by the vision of a fillet steak or a bar of chocolate. In the cool of the evening I would sink into despair, reaching the verge of suicide, convinced that human happiness was the illusion of fools, no sooner grasped than lost. But when the walk ended I was filled with a wonderful calmness and serenity, far greater than anything I had experienced with drugs.

When I returned from India there was a place waiting for me at Durham University to study anthropology. I tried to study for a year but I couldn't settle and spent all my time in the oriental section of the university library reading Hindu and Buddhist scriptures. Then I begged my father for more cash and returned to India, this time in search of a guru to whom I could surrender myself. To achieve that interior happiness which I had seen in the holy men, I needed my own holy man to show me how. It never struck me that I could find such a teacher here in Britain – India seemed the natural place to look.

Soon after arriving in India this second time, I was taken to visit a Christian ashram, a small community of Indian Christian monks. The community was organised in the same way as the normal Hindu ashram which develops around a guru, but in this case the guru was Jesus Christ. This may seem surprising, but it was one of a number of ashrams founded in India in the 1920s and 1930s in order to develop a Hindu form of Christianity more accessible to the ordinary Indian. On the insistence of the monks I stayed in the ashram almost a year, building myself a small hut to live in. I still considered myself an agnostic but believed that as an agnostic I could nevertheless share the happiness which religious people enjoy. The monks laughed at my agnosticism as a silly intellectual hang-up, 'None of us have perfect knowledge', they said, 'so we are all agnostics'. I joined in their worship and meditation, and with their help began to study the gospels.

At first the continual references to God and to Heaven interfered, but I decided to treat God as a synonym for human fulfilment, and Heaven as the joy of that fulfilment. Now I could read the gospels straight through like a book and I was captivated. I fell in love with the simple carpenter who abandoned his job and started wandering from village to village, begging for food and shelter, healing the sick and teaching those who asked for guidance. I could see the grubby robes clinging to his thin sweaty body; I could feel the soothing calm of his presence; I could hear the gentle laughter in his voice. The reality which I had found in the Indian holy men shone brilliantly through the pages of the gospels. My guru had been under my nose, or rather beside me on the bookshelf, throughout my life.

But I still lacked courage; I wasn't certain. I was the bride-to-be having doubts on the night before the wedding. So I decided to try an experiment. I would make Jesus my guru for a test period of six months. During that time I would study his teachings in detail and follow his instructions, regardless of whether I fully understood or agreed with them. Then at the end of the six months I would review my progress. I never made that review. Long before the six months were up I knew I had found my guru. And as I clumsily tried to follow his instructions on prayer, I found also my God.

Like all gurus, Jesus instructs his disciples to join together and form a community. I spent three years back in England hovering on the edge, trying to resist that instruction, praying and worshipping in lots of churches, but committing myself to none. I went each Sunday to receive the Eucharist, to be joined physically to my guru, but I refused to join the community. Eventually, when my wife and I settled in a town in north Lancashire, I took the plunge. I am now an Anglican, an active member as they say, playing my part in the worship and the committees and all the various activities which hold the human institution together.

To an outsider my church, like many others, shows little of the spiritual wealth which it possesses. A casual observer on a Sunday morning sees only expressionless faces and almost motionless bodies. But I have learned now to sense the spiritual wealth that is within. For among those motionless bodies, amidst the people who still go to church each week out of sheer habit, there are saints – far more numerous and more saintly than I had imagined. Casual aquaintance reveals nothing of this. The depth of love and prayer is hidden in the warm silence of their hearts and only prolonged contact reveals it to an untrained novice like myself.

I now believe that my contemporaries are rejecting the wealth and the doctrine of enlightened self-interest which they were heir to – they are spitting out the silver spoon. During the past century or more the church has been in a recession with congregations slumping; but if the church chooses to respond all this may change as young people instinctively turn inwards towards the human spirit. The prolonged recession will turn into a boom. If the church can show the world its hidden spiritual riches young people will fall over themselves to grab a share. Western Christianity must first, I believe, rid itself of its age old obsession with intellectual rigour. Instead of being all things to all men it still addresses itself only to those who can utter certain credal formulae. The priests and theologians are still bound up in defining precisely what Christians should not believe, and so it makes the agnosticism of the present generation into an almost impossible stumbling block which only a few lucky people like myself can overcome. This stumbling block is false; Jesus speaks to all men whatever their initial beliefs and prejudices and all men want to be happy. Jesus is first and foremost a teacher of human happiness. The duty to proclaim this fact rests with ordinary Christians in the ordinary humdrum parishes, and so it is with them that I identify myself.

I long for the Church to shine with the joy and happiness of its guru, for Christians to bask in the light and warmth of the Resurrection – for them to reveal to the world that the Christian life is truly more pleasurable than that of the consumer society. This perhaps is just beginning to happen – and when it does the disillusioned refugees of affluence will fill the Church's pews.

SATISH KUMAR
JOURNEY TO THE WEST

I come from the desert area of Rajestan in India and at the age of nine I became a wandering monk. From the very earliest years I felt a sort of loneliness in the world around me. I felt a sort of alien, I did not fit, I did not belong to this place. At the age of nine I left my mother and my village and accepted the guru of the monks of the Jain religion. From now on I was a begging monk and I travelled on foot, walking from place to place.

The circumstances of life have changed but ever since that time I have continued to be a beggar and a wanderer. Everything that I have learned in life, I have learned in wandering. The Jain religion says that we can escape the suffering of life only by consciously accepting suffering and going through it; by being totally humble, non-violent, learning to be detached. So the monks' life is not easy – my guru used to tell a story of Mahavir, the founder of Jainism, to illustrate how to accept difficulties. Mahavir believed that begging should not be easy and made a vow that he would only accept food from a princess. This princess, he decided, would have to have been sold into bondage and chained by the foot so that one foot was outside the house and one foot inside. And there must also be tears in her eyes and she must offer him soaked beans on a bamboo plate. These conditions made his task as a beggar very difficult – he had to travel with nothing, expecting nothing. Inevitably Mahavir had to go without food for very many days and many nights until at last the day came when he saw, sitting in the doorway of a rich man's house, a woman whom he recognised as the daughter of a conquered King. The rich man had left her chained in the porch. When she saw Mahavir coming she recognised him and rejoiced calling out 'Oh Lord Mahavir, in my pain and misfortune you have found me, teach me the way to liberation. I have nothing but soaked beans to offer you, accept them and give me your blessing.' Mahavir looked into her face but she was smiling, there were no tears there, so he turned away. At this the princess wept and called out 'Everyone has deserted me and now even you refuse my offering, to whom shall I look in this world'. Then Mahavir turned to her again and seeing tears in her eyes he put both hands together and accepted the food.

Of course I did not understand this way of life when I started. I asked questions but my guru said, 'There is no answer that can be given by word of mouth. If I give you a verbal answer that will create more questions in the end'. He said 'Your full attention should be inside you, work within, work on your inner self, what is happening in your mind, in your heart, what sort of anger, what sort of hope, what sort of greed, what sort of attachment are coming up within you'. And all these passions were in me and I felt them – the life of the monk makes the inner life very strong. I learned that begging is much more difficult than giving. You have to deny your greed and even if somebody says 'No, go away, you are a strong young man why are you begging?' still you beg. It is very difficult to be humble and not angry. The begging monk can become very humble, very unassuming. My teacher said, 'Go like a honey bee from flower to flower never taking too much in one place.'

I was a monk for nine years but I still felt some lack of belong-ingness. The company of monks was narrow, too limiting. The ideas and the path I was following was right, but it was not big enough. So I joined the walking group of people who were begging the rich to give land to the poor. And this continued my walking and begging in a broader context.

It was at this time in India that I heard of another kind of walk-ing and begging going on thousands of miles away – in the west at Aldermaston. This time people were begging for peace. We discussed these events especially when Bertrand Russell was arrested and I thought if Russell is willing to walk for peace at his age, what sort of things could we do as young people? So the longing to be wandering came to me again and with a friend I decided to walk to the west around the world.

It was to be a walk for peace but really peace was a kind of excuse. At heart was again the longing to be free, to wander, to be in the wide world without any labels, without any cultural or religious barriers. Often in life we find some excuse to do something we already want to do. So I decided to walk round the world for peace and at the centre was this desire to experience the unity of the world and myself. Still looking for belongingness, I wished no barriers. My teacher told me to walk without money. He said, 'Money is the greatest barrier between you and people. If you are tired, with money you will go to sleep in a hotel and eat in a restaurant and walk away. If you have no money you will be forced to find somebody who can give you food and shelter and to prove yourself a worthy guest – this way you will meet people.'

So we set out. We pledged ourselves to depend only on the people we met, to travel without food or money and for transport use only our two legs. Of course it is easy enough to walk waving a banner for peace but the very first border we came to challenged our intentions. India and Pakistan have had many problems between them, so this is what we said to those who asked us who we were and where we came from: 'We are human beings first and last, our religion is our faith in humanity and there can be no religion greater than that. If we call ourselves Indians we will meet Pakistanis. If we go as Hindus we will meet Christians or Muslims. If we go as socialists we will meet capitalists. If we go as human beings we will meet human beings everywhere'.

When we came to the Khyber Pass we came across the emblems of military life and ironically we were given a military escort to protect us from the Pathan tribesmen, who have a ferocious reputation. And yet the tribesmen said to us 'Much malicious propaganda is made against us, but if a guest comes to us, God comes in him. We carry arms to protect our guests, even at the cost of our lives.' And so we passed on into Afghanistan. Deserts and mountains, our feet blistered, hungry and thirsty, we always found hospitality in the evenings as we sat drinking tea with the people. Going into an unknown world and confronting it without a penny in my pocket, so that I had no support or external security, meant that all the differences between rich and poor, educated and illiterate, vanished and the real life beneath these divisions emerged. As a wanderer I was free of shadows of the past, nobody knew of me when we met and I didn't know of them. We were all reduced to our real human size.

We passed on into Iran and again there was hospitality everywhere. Many ordinary people tried to give us gifts, as did the Shah of Persia who granted us an audience. He was most surprised when we wouldn't accept money to help us on our way. And so by way of the Caspian Sea we came to southern Russia. Here we were invited to tell of our peace walk in a tea factory. Afterwards one worker ran up to us and gave us four packets of tea saying 'We agree with every word you say. Here are four packets of our tea. Please give one each to Kruschev, de Gaulle, Macmillan and Kennedy. Tell them if they think of pushing the button to drop their bombs, they should stop a moment and have a fresh cup of tea from these packets. That will give them a chance to remember that the simple workers of the world want bread and not bombs, life and not death.' Another time in Russia we spent an evening in a village where the people pressed us to drink wine and dance. I said we do not drink but they said, water is for washing, wine is for drinking and so we drank with them and I was carried away and sang one of the songs of Tagore.

But now the western mind began to influence our walk. The winter was approaching and the Russian authorities insisted on flying us over the mountains, although we wished to travel on foot. Actually they played a well-meaning trick on us and flew us all the way to Moscow. Our walk continued all over the west and by now I had learned an important lesson. I discovered that there is a unity between the ordinary people of different nations.

There was no difference between me and the Iranians or me and the Russians. We are one. The difference between a Jain and a Christian is only superficial. Being a Hindu, a communist, a Jain, a Christian is only an excuse – if an important excuse – because we want to experience something beyond our life. So we read the Bible or chant Hare Krishna to experience something deeper than words. I began to experience this oneness, this unity of people, even the physical unity of everything.

Walking taught me that I and the earth are one thing – we are no more separate than my hand is different from me. So this experience of unity was the deep one, the main experience. Now I belonged, to everyone, everything, everywhere. In the years since then I have been involved in many different activities and I have learned something in the west which is expressed so well in a traditional Indian story about how we seek truth. 'Once a group of men were told that a certain animal was in a dark room and they were invited to inspect it through very small windows. One of the men saw a thin hanging rope-like apparition. He walked away and told his friends "The strange animal is like a crusty worm". Another of the men saw through his window a flat rugged area of nondescript colour. He told his friends later "The beast is of a most unusual flat nature". Others looked through other windows and all had different things to report. Their friends, who had not themselves seen through the windows, argued with other groups on behalf of their view. Some people even tried to add all the different views together. But they never managed to imagine the whole animal – the total elephant.' This story really is the example of what I have found here. The western mind is very analytical. The west specialises in analysis – it may even be a disease. There are problems, with economics, social questions, environment, personal matters, and there are specialists for all these things. But everything is interrelated. You cannot have a good ecology without a good economy, a good economy without good politics, good politics without good psychology, psychology without sex, sex without love, love without the spiritual realisation. And you cannot have this realisation without God – everything is connected and cannot be separated.

This interrelatedness I learned by living in the west. That may seem a paradox. The west is always specialising and yet I found the unity through this. Perhaps I can explain by saying that in India I did not realise this because it never has to be said. There is not so much analysis or separating of things – so you take everything for granted. But here, seeing analysis, I noticed the totality.

So my search for belongingness has caused me to be a wanderer and wandering has brought me to this unity, this sense of belonging to everything. This is my way, yours may be different. For me the journey which takes place outside actually is an inside journey. The inside journey is a journey to discover and realise oneself, to recognise the diversity and find the unity underlying· The self and the not-self are one.

BEL MOONEY

A BIRTH OF HOPE

I don't remember ever thinking about having children. Like many women, I just assumed that one day it would happen. Perhaps I romanticised the clean white bundles in the babyfood advertisements or fantasised about the awesome, primitive moment of birth. Sometimes I feared pain and responsibility. If ever I did think, considering the implications of bringing a life into the world, it was from a safe distance. Around me in the streets I saw them – young girls with swelling stomachs, smiling mums with loaded carrycots, anxious women with shopping bags and toddlers clinging to their coats. They existed across a gulf.

Then, when I first became pregnant, I pretended it wasn't happening – refusing to rest, working hard, fearing the loss of my freedom. When my son Daniel was born I felt calm for the first time in years and I loved him of course. I didn't ever think about what he was doing there in my arms.

I have always made plans and expected the world to fit in with them. So a year later I got pregnant again as a matter of course, deciding that two children with a gap of two years is the ideal. This time I did stay at home and rest for the nine months – so the waiting seemed longer; and all the time I was convinced that the child inside me was a boy. It was a boy. On 26 November 1975, after sixteen hours of labour, he was born, very small, perfectly formed – but dead. It was what they call a stillbirth.

I could never have predicted that I should feel such love and loss for someone I had never met. The very shock of that emotion was isolating – though I was lucky in being able to share my grief with a husband who participated equally in its intensity.

But other people, meaning to be encouraging, said: 'You can always have another one.' It outraged me. If my husband had died they would not have said, 'Oh you can always marry again'. Those who have escaped the experience of stillbirth cannot approach its meaning; that the baby is a real person to the mother who bore him. Yet if you stop to think about that, of course, it must be true. The unborn child is part of the rhythm of your being, living in you, through you, with you. For nine months you are prepared to be a mother. Without that baby you are still a mother – ready and cheated. Nature is not kind, so your body carries on as normal, filling painful breasts with milk to feed the child who is not there.

I felt that I had failed as a woman, hating my body as a defective machine. The anger was frightening. I said that children mean nothing but grief; that marriage itself, being a cause of children, was a source of pain. With the anger came great guilt. With the sense of physical uselessness came a feeling of moral responsibility. So I protested that I had not been wicked, that I did not deserve what had happened. I screamed, 'Why should I be punished?' The words assumed an area of responsibility far deeper than the physical; not only had I failed to fulfil my sexual function, I had failed as a human being. Trying to find a reason for the irrational, you turn upon yourself and the self-hatred can last for months. What makes it worse is that it's impossible to express. Though kind, people think you should 'pull yourself together', not mention what torments you. Yet the bereaved long to talk. For me, talking about the baby proved he existed, and sharing that fact with others gave it importance.

Two weeks afterwards I wrote down how I felt and the final article was published in *The Guardian*. Then I no longer felt isolated. In deciding that the personal event was not private, I discovered that my emotions – including that inexpressible guilt – were shared. I knew that stillbirths are relatively common – about one in every sixty deliveries – but not that my own feelings were quite ordinary. The dozens of letters I received after the article made me cry with a relief that was close to joy that a shared experience could bring people who had never met as close as my unborn child had been to me.

Grief persists – for weeks, months, years. Certain thoughts or objects can quickly probe it, like the sudden opening of a half-healed wound. Or it can be a dull throb, a dark vein running under the skin, a perpetual awareness of pain. The bereaved need to feel that others know. But stillbirth is especially hard to understand. At the death of your grandparents you may remember with guilt the irritation you felt at their old age. If your mother dies you may recall with tenderness a small woman with a shopping bag. If your brother dies you can remember the childhood fights, rivalry, companionship. You can remember Christmases and conflict, good and bad. But when a child is born dead there is nothing. The world can remember nothing. And for you, the gap in the womb is replaced by an emptiness in your arms, and all the nine months' waiting comes to this terrible void, the cessation of hope. You are vacant and deficient – a walking vacuum, who mourns a non-person.

More than that, a child born dead is an overturning of the natural order of events: we live and *then* we die. So in hospital the doctors and nurses cannot cope. It is not part of their function in the maternity ward to ease death into the world. You are an outsider, not really a mother, whose cries must be stilled with sedatives. Then the requirements of bureaucracy make you feel the more freakish. One rainy day my husband had to go to the Registrar of Births, Marriages and Deaths to record the event that was none of these, to witness the facts written out in the special book they keep hidden in a drawer for the Stillbirths. For you are not recording a birth, or a death, but both at once. It is the ultimate contradiction. I felt I had created death.

I have always loved poetry and part of a poem by T. S. Eliot helped me cope with this confusion. It is from *The Journey of the Magi*, where the pagan kings remember the nativity:

All this was a long time ago, I remember,
And I would do it again, but set down

This set down
This: were we led all that way for
Birth or Death? There was a Birth, certainly,
We had evidence and no doubt. I had seen birth
and death
But had thought they were different; this Birth was
Hard and bitter agony for us, like Death, our death.

T. S. Eliot's pen is actually about the human capacity to be utterly changed by an experience, so that it calls into question everything you have been, all that you believe in. That change involves a form of death. When my son died, a part of me died with him, because (as anyone who has been bereaved knows) afterwards your life can never be the same again. Why should it. Why should we turn away from that knowledge? Why should we immediately pull back the blanket of 'normality' around us, to keep out the cold? I choose to confront the cold, because I believe, with some pride, that human beings have the strength to bear what seems unbearable, and grow in the attempt. When I wrote the newspaper article I ended with these words: 'I do not wish to get over his loss; nor do I wish to replace him with more children. I simply wish that this life and death should be absorbed into my own, enlarging and deepening in perception.'

I would still wish that. But a year later, reality is bleaker – I know it is not so easy. There are still the tears at the sight of a baby the age he would have been; the unbidden painful image of the cot we took out of the cupboard and had to put back again. I'm afraid there are no moments of sudden revelation, there is simply a long, slow process of self-knowledge, an unwilling acceptance of grief.

Sylvia Plath wrote a poem for radio about the experience of three women in a maternity ward: including a woman whose child is stillborn. Her lines are full of winter, of emptiness. Then at the end the note changes and we witness in her the birth of hope:

I am at home in the lamplight. The evenings
    are lengthening.
I am mending a silk slip; my husband is reading.
How beautifully the light includes these things.
There is a kind of smoke in the spring air,
A smoke that takes the parks, the little statues
With pinkness, as if a tenderness awoke,
A tenderness that did not tire, something healing.

Strangely, the acceptance of impermanence, of imperfection, is healing. Though at first you scream out 'Why me?', you stop and think one day, 'Why *not* me?'.

Bereavement can leave you bleak and bitter, but it can also make you perceive, for the first time, your own ordinary, vulnerable humanity. Our second son was conceived, existed, then died – it was simply a telescoping, a speeding-up of the process we all endure, though pure, and without the disappointments of age. Realising the reality of his brief existence made me think of him as, somehow, separate – not a cuddly, romantic fantasy; not as a unit in a nuclear family; not someone to satisfy the expectations of grandparents; not (above all) as an adjunct to my world; but himself, a separate and unique soul. Perceiving the individuality of the unborn child, made me think of other lives, of the masses of people around me, as important individuals. And it intensified for me the preciousness of all those individual lives. For when those mothers wrote to me, and I cried for their children as for my own, neither they nor I were being morbid, dwelling upon death. On the contrary, I am celebrating life; the life that begins in the womb; the life of the mind that goes on coping, trying to understand the pain that surrounds it; and the life of the imagination which feels, like John Donne, that 'any man's death diminishes me'.

It is too glib to talk of good coming out of suffering, for there are some things no one should have to bear – man-made pain which is pure evil. There is no place for easy consolation for the mothers of children killed by bombs or bullets or famine or fanaticism. There is a place there for anger. But the ordinary undramatic thing that happened to me, the sadness that has to be accepted, that can be enlarging. When I am making a meal, or working at my typewriter, or listening to news of far worse things, I remember it. When I am playing in the garden with Daniel, hearing him laugh, feeling furious when he whines or realising that I can no longer call him 'my baby' I am conscious of two things. First, that there were two children, as I planned, and the other one is an ever-present reality. Second, that Daniel is an individual. From the beginning he has possessed his own private reality, just as the other one had. I do not own him, I want to share him with the world and let others know the quiet delight I feel in his presence. And there is another thing. I may not have another child. But how can Daniel be an 'only child', when the world is full of children? The death of his brother made me love all human life more precisely. And it is that opening-up, that feeling of being part of a whole, which makes the many moments of present joy all the more intense.

JOHN WYATT

WRAP ME AROUND WITH TREES

I have been a countryman all my life. I have had a
straw in my mouth, a stick in my hand, and a dog at my heels
almost from the day I could walk. As a child this made me a pe-
culiar misfit, because I was born in a terraced house next door to
the co-op, opposite a coal-tip, among the Lancashire cotton mill
chimneys, and around the corner from a tripe, cowheel and
blackpudding works. I'm not complaining. I couldn't have
chosen better parents; and the townsfolk, united by hard times,
were warm and friendly. But there were no gardens; not a single
tree; hardly a blade of grass. And everything was covered with
industrial grime.

Even as a boy, I was fascinated by nature. As soon as I was able
to wander I was off to a local wood and when I joined the scouts I
was introduced to the Peak District, only a short journey away. I
read a lot about animals and birds and plants and tramped for
miles in search of them. Then the scout troop went to camp in the
Lake District. We camped in a wood and it was a revelation. For
the first time I saw all the plants and the birds and the animals
beginning to fit into a pattern. I sat under a yew tree overlooking
a rippling sea of leaves and bracken. Looking over to the lake
and the moor and the mountains behind I felt a surge of
excitement. I am quite sure I wasn't stirred by the obvious
beauty of it. That must have come later. The pieces I had read
about were coming together and I was really only on the edge.
The pattern went on all around and above and at my feet.
Nature shouted of wholeness. I was alive for the first time. I
found I was part of this pattern and I wanted to go on belonging –
and where I found I belonged more and more was among the trees.

One way and another trees became to me a point of reference for the rest of my life – wrap a wood around me and I'm happy. I suppose most of us have a romantic idea of living in the country. But if my early notions were romantic I soon had them knocked out of me. I got my first job in the Lake District in my teens and did manual work, learning to swing an axe, use a billhook, a pick and a sledge hammer until my blisters had blisters; cross-cutting until my muscles cried out for mercy. It was the right initiation. I soon learned that nature was not something that you just read about and had great thoughts about. It slashed my legs; it tore my clothes, nipped my fingers, covered me with muck; wet me through; kicked, bit, stung, irritated, froze and burnt me.

I may once have felt that cows were loveable creatures providing milk out of kindness. After mucking out their shippon I soon understood with some feeling the meaning of the countryman's expression 'as rare as a constipated cow'. And sheep and lambs I may have felt looked decorative on the rural scene, but I soon learned how incredibly difficult it is to keep them out of a plantation. If they get in it takes three Olympic gold medallists to clear a five-acre plot. I could have borrowed a dog but I could never master the art of putting frozen fingers in my mouth, whistling, and swearing at the same time. Buttercups I may have once thought charming, giving a lovely splash of colour to the countryside. But, when dragging out the spreading roots of the stuff, like Wordsworth, I knew that the meanest flower that blows can give thoughts that do often lie too deep for tears.

I remember listening to a colleague lecturing about the Lake District, saying: 'Of course it rains quite a bit in the holiday season, but even the rain has its romantic charm.' I had to bite my tongue. For here was a friend who had just admitted that he had never had to stay in the rain longer than it takes to put up an umbrella. There is nothing romantic about working in the rain with wet feet, mud up to your armpits and your finger-ends dropping off with cold, with romantic rain running down the neck-collar, trickling down your vest and into your romantic underpants.

It may seem ridiculous to you but after a while of living in a wood, trees became to me, in form and character, more real than people. The shape of an individual tree tells its entire life story. Unlike a human, whose shape is already fixed in embryo, by comparison a ripe tree seed is only a general proposition; soul rather than image. Once the shoots and roots burst outwards the plant is subject only to the general law which governs its species, and the rest of its life is what its own immediate environment and climate make of it. It must fight for its own share of light and nourishment. In the bareness of winter the full story can be read. Each tree is a tight colony of plants grouped around the dead inherited heartwood, the spine, and thrusting for life. Every turn and bulge of the tree trunk, every buttress on its bole, all the stretch of root and branch, is a gesture of aggression or defence. A tree is a battle hymn. If you put your ear to the trunk on a windy day, you can hear it.

Every tree group is sharing light and nourishment and the shape of each tree is modified to accommodate its neighbour. Neighbours of the same species may even fuse their roots together to share the minerals and moisture. Nothing is lost in a wood. Nature adjusts the balance. A tree falls and in the shafts of light allowed in the canopy a hundred dormant tree seedlings explode into new life, heralded by a burst of flowers. I felt that I really belonged in this sensibly ordered community.

Probably most people's first contact with a wood is discouraging. It is very easy to lose all sense of direction and to walk in circles. In very wet weather trees have a playful habit of pretending to offer shelter, then suddenly channelling jets of water down your neck. Branches thump you on the head and twigs do their best to scratch your eyes out. And although the woods are more or less dead quiet for much of the time, the dawn chorus of birds of a spring morning murders sleep. It is like trying to kip in Huddersfield town hall with the choral society belting out the Hallelujah chorus.

Then there is the slight feeling of uneasiness that one occasionally fears. A fringe of the wood is all right perhaps, but deep down in the heart of it the trees seem almost to move around you and close in. Then in the utter silence in these depths one can feel, as I sometimes could, a sense of strange dread.

Little wonder that religion was born in the woods. The inspiration of those who made civilisation's first temples and churches all over the world was the forest. You can see it in the pillars, the vaulted roofs, the decorated ceilings, even in the filtering light from stained-glass windows. For the ancient gods walked in the woods and they speak in the terrible silence. If you are brave enough to walk into the depths alone you may walk through the trees, down the naves, and suddenly, in this place of long trunks, great brooding boughs, and below this spreading canopy, you are about the altar. For that moment you are really alone, more lonely than you have ever been. You don't know why this is the place – this glade of all glades. But you are suddenly an intruder. You walked in more or less master of your own fate. You had purpose. You suddenly forget what it was. For that voice says 'Be still' and if you have the courage to heed and wait, you might be on the brink of knowing.

I lived with this feeling, a sort of exhilarating dread. As I began to know the trees, the individuals and the families and how they share their lives together, I was going on from the point where I was first beginning to see this great pattern of nature in four dimensions, not only in the woods, but wherever I stood. It was all the more obvious when I could stand high, looking into the depths of the valley and the shining levels of the lake and up into the mountain peaks. On from the tree at my elbow into the hazy blue horizon. And I was looking then through eternity. For the rock on which I stood was laid down in a sea 400 million years ago. The craggy mountains ahead were spewed out of volcanic vents 500 million years ago. The landscape as I saw it was carved out by the great rivers of ice in the last half million years. And the whole was living and breathing. Nothing had finished. The mountains were crumbling into the valleys and the fragments washed down into the shallowing lakes. But down in the great earth depths the lungs rose and fell. Some day the mountains might rise again and the woods and lakes vanish under rock and dust. But in the great time scale; not in the human flicker. Yet humanity, appearing in the last blink of an eye, was bound up with it and was wholly part of it. And I was part of it.

I was so absorbed in this awakening of consciousness that I never felt alone in my solitude. For true solitude is not loneliness. It is a great oneness. One with everything: the cool grass, the animals and birds, the glade, the wood, the hills, the lakes, the countryside, the thin envelope of gas which gives our world life: the planet, the galaxy, the universe. It was easy in my solitude, to sense the motion and the spirit that rolls through all things. In the thrusting life of the wood I could see the human situation and my own. I was, I suppose, looking for myself in my solitude. If I didn't entirely succeed at least I found where I fitted – somewhere in this great wholeness, this balanced order, there was a niche – and that was an exciting start. If I lost my bearings I had only to return to the trees.

Wherever I am – on the fell, by the lake shore, on the lanes, or in the woods, or even in the city park – I can feel every day as Jacob did and think:

How dreadful is this place.
This is none other than the house of God.
This is the gate of heaven.

JACK BURTON
MY CAB IS MY CLOISTER

In my wardrobe at home hang two uniforms. One is like a long black dress with a white collar: the other is blue and has a badge with a number. People have suggested that I lead a double life, for I am both an ordained Methodist minister and a bus driver. Sometimes I climb into a pulpit and preach sermons and sometimes I climb into a cab. Sometimes I meet people in church as a minister and sometimes I drive a double-decker through the rush-hour. Sometimes I pray, and sometimes I moan at my conductor when he forgets to change the screen!

I was converted to the Christian faith as a boy of fifteen. What complex adolescent drives were involved in that event I don't know: what nobody can deny is that the next twenty years were shaped and determined by that teenage experience. I was so eager to share my faith that eventually I entered the ministry and for five years served in the traditional work. But gradually I began to feel a deep and depressing sense of isolation, futility and unreality. I prepared challenging sermons, but the same little groups heard them each week; I posted notices saying, 'Everybody welcome', but no one paid much attention. I felt I had been shunted off the main line of the world's life and into a siding. I felt that the devil had laughed when I entered the ministry because he knew I would no longer be in the thick of things. I vowed he would not have the last laugh. It was Dietrich Bonhoeffer who wrote: 'Luther's return from the cloister to the world was the worst blow the devil had suffered since the days of early Christianity. The renunciation he made when he became a monk was child's play compared with that which he had to make when he returned to the world.' That is rather how I felt!

I asked the church if I might remain a minister but earn my living at manual work. It was a tough struggle, but permission was finally granted. The isolation and futility ceased. Once more I was at large. I was eager to meet all sorts of people, not just the small circle of church people I met as a minister. And I have learned more since I have been on the buses than ever before. It is through my work as a bus driver that I meet many people.

The first person I meet in the morning is my conductor, Tony. He's not too keen on religion, so we don't discuss it; he prefers football. While he writes out his waybill for the day's journeys, I book on for duty, find our bus, check the water, put the destination on the screen, and then we're off. Often people ask why I didn't become a conductor. I am not sure I would have enough patience to do that job well. In any case, the conductor is far too busy to offer a text with every ticket!

At first I wondered if I would be accepted, but the people I work with take me as I am. They don't seem to think of me as a parson disguised as a human being. The novelty of having a parson around has long since worn off and I feel I am trusted. I enjoy the life, the jokes and banter. Take Mick, a conductor; he is a qualified football referee in the local Sunday league. He regards my Sunday activities as being on a par with his own, and each Monday he insists on comparing notes. 'Did you have a match yesterday, Jack?' 'I had two! One at eleven, and a floodlit fixture at night.' 'Will you be buying any new choirboys before the transfer deadline?' 'I don't think so, although we could do with a new verger.' 'Most teams could, but there aren't many good virgins about.' 'I said *verger*!'

I no longer feel caged behind a church wall. I have experienced an extraordinary sense of companionship and affection and I have talked and listened to many people. The demands on my time are heavy, but it all seems worthwhile. This is much closer to what I imagined the ministry to be.

Many busmen have attended my services occasionally and I have married busmen, buried busmen, and baptised busmen's babies! But I've made no converts, no new church members; I very much wish I had. But to my horror, I have realised that it doesn't really matter. The purpose of my ministry is not simply to herd people into a building, but to encourage them to look at the world a little differently, to raise questions and suggest ideas that widen horizons. More than anything I wish we could feel the wonder of love – a love that has to take risks. That is why I enjoy meeting people in the pub. People find it so hard to truly meet! We protect ourselves and hide behind fronts and barriers because we are afraid others might discover too much about us and as a result we imprison ourselves in isolation and loneliness. Some of that withdrawn secrecy evaporates in the pub. As we relax and become slightly less tense and on guard, the real 'us' filters closer to the surface and, perhaps only briefly, true meeting begins to take place.

I have had superb discussions in the pub – not point-scoring debates, but ordinary people daring to ask real questions. I remember one man who only wanted to know the time, and twenty minutes later he was still asserting the impossibility of the resurrection! I don't go to the pub deliberately to evangelise, though give me half a chance and I'll take it. Like everyone else, I go to enjoy a drink and to forget the pressures for an hour and I like the laughter and the gossip. But for me Christ is in the pub. I must admit that often I've felt his presence more powerfully in a pub than in many churches I've been to. When people admit their weaknesses and worries and hopes and delights, with simplicity and honesty, I feel we are no longer meeting alone. We are meeting in the strong presence of Christ, who prompts all truthfulness and idealism. Does that sound like a bit from a sermon? Well, I'm not going to apologise. I do believe that in meeting people we are meeting God. I think back to that sense of isolation which once sapped the gladness from life, and I am grateful to be back in the world.

But something else has happened since I started on the buses. Take my cab, for example. This seems an immense paradox, but my cab is like a cloister. Although it is from my cab that I see the world it is also the place where I sit in solitude for hours and where all kinds of thoughts flash through my mind. In the middle of the rush-hour, I sit in a monastic cell! And as I stare through the windscreen I have begun to see clues and signs of God's presence everywhere. I draw up at a bus-stop and see small children; people going to work; pretty girls; elderly people, their faces lined with experience but who themselves once were children and youngsters. I wonder at the mystery of time – of birth and growth and decay. And I drive past ancient buildings which have watched not only buses but waggons and coaches and horses and, in other ages, have sheltered men who have brooded over the same mysteries of existence which perplex us. The castle, the medieval churches, the cathedral whose architecture is in itself a form of praise. We are like actors in a timeless pageant.

And I sing in the cab, I roar away to my heart's content, the sound mostly drowned by the roar of a six-cylinder diesel engine. Sometimes Tony can hear and bangs on the window to silence me, but I ignore him! Music is so important. More than anything else apart from sex, it has the powerful ability to pierce the veil between the seen and unseen worlds. My tastes are varied, but often I sing English church music. In my mind I hear the choirs singing and I join in heartily and without inhibition.

Sometimes we drive on a country route and it is from my cab, too, that I notice the beauty of the world, the splendour and wonder of the creation: rainbows, cloud patterns, sunrises, slanting rain, hoar frost, changing seasons. I think of the Psalms:

O praise the Lord of heaven: praise him in the height
Praise him, all ye angels of his: praise him all his host.
Praise him, sun and moon: praise him, all ye stars and light.
Praise him, all ye heavens: and ye waters that are above the
    heavens.
Let them praise the Name of the Lord: for he spake the word,
    and they were made; he commanded, and they were
    created.

The wonders of modern technology have made us incredibly blasé about the astonishing creation of which we form a part.

There is a rhythm to the cosmos: seasons, tides, night and day, pulse and heartbeat, life and death. To be aware of nature is to be aware of the God who moves through nature. A pattern begins to emerge: people, laughter, warmth, history, music, nature merge into a rich mosaic of daily life. To which I personally must add family. I have two energetic daughters, Linda and Jeanette, who wreak havoc in our sitting room in three minutes flat. My son, Trevor, is head chorister in the cathedral choir and seems to work shifts almost as complicated as my own. And presiding over this whirlwind of activity is my wife, Molly, without whom our family would produce no books, no programmes, no hymns, nor anything of note. How she keeps control of our household I shall simply never understand.

Life is so rich! There is suffering and pain, but there is also gladness, and celebration, and friendship, and love. For me, all these threads are drawn together in worship – especially in the communion. Church services are occasions when I attempt formally, consciously and deliberately to respond to that spirit, God, mystery, sense of 'otherness' – call it what you will – which I encounter and experience in every part of life.

My years as a bus driver have taught me a great deal, but above all they have taught me these two things. First, there is a glorious catholicity about human life, in which work, sex, religion, humour, nature, sport, poetry, architecture, music, history, love and friendship form part of one brilliant whole, and are not isolated fragments of awareness. And second that for most of us, God is not likely to be experienced by turning away from the world, but by taking hold of life and revelling in its rough-and-tumble, and by developing wide interests and living deeply. God is not confined to the church. He, too, is at large, and the whole creation is the arena of his activity.

MAEVE BINCHY

NOBODY IS WATCHING ME

I am a foot taller than Napolean and twice the weight of Twiggy; on my only visit to a beautician the woman said that she found my face a challenge. Not long ago I choked in a restaurant so badly that everyone there had to come and bang me on the back. And yet despite all these social disadvantages I feel cheerful, happy, confident and secure.

I work for a daily newspaper and so get to a lot of places I would never otherwise see. This year I went to Ascot to write about the people there and I saw something that made me realise the folly of trying to conform, of trying to be better than anyone else. There was a small plump woman, all dressed up, huge hat, dress with pink butterflies, long white gloves. She had obviously been looking forward to the day out for ages, and to make herself even more elegant she had taken along one of those shooting-stick things. But because she was so plump, sitting on this shooting-stick had embedded it in the ground and when she wanted to move off she couldn't dislodge it. She tugged and wrenched, tears of rage in her eyes. When the final tug dislodged it, she crashed to the ground with a mighty thud. I saw her walk away, her day, and possibly her life, had been ruined. She had made a public spectacle of herself, she had impressed nobody. In her own sad red eyes she was a failure. But actually I don't think anybody but me had seen her at all.

I remember it well when I was like that myself. That was in the days before I saw the great light of reason and learned the eye-opening fact that nobody really cares what you do from one end of the day to the other. There were years and years of trying to be like other people, praying that nobody would notice I wasn't as good as the herd; endless and useless speculation about what people might be thinking about me; hours of worrying about that when now I know they weren't thinking about me at all.

At my convent school I had two big worries. One was about becoming a saint which I was very anxious to do, but I didn't want to let the other girls know in case they would laugh at me. The other worry was that I was hopeless at games and everybody else seemed to be very good at them. The games problem was more worrying. To this day I can never see a hockey game without remembering the shame I felt at not being able to thunder up and down at speed and the horrible cry of the hockey captain who would bellow: 'Oh Maeve you're letting the team down again'. The sainthood ambition was beset with difficulties too. I had it firmly fixed in my mind that God was a jovial Irishman with a moustache, a sense of humour exactly parallel to my own, and had a special high place waiting for me When The Time Came. I used to drop into the church regularly to let Him know that everything was going according to plan and that if He didn't mind I'd be very happy not to undergo martyrdom, but be a peaceful kind of saint like St Teresa of Lisierx, but of course that if he thought it had to be martyrdom well that's what it had better be.

I suppose there were some people who grew up calmly and without hassle and confusions in the 1950s. Nostalgic films of the decade show everyone jiving and rock-and-rolling and absorbing an American culture quite happily. It is always seen now as the time when people forgot post-war gloom, and started to live again; started to be happy and carefree; started to love living. But there must have been people like myself as well. Terribly worried because I wasn't as thin and energetic as all these dancers and co-eds and bobby-soxers I saw in the movies and eating more and more chocolate cakes to get over the misery of it.

I remember the agony of my first dance, something that is always meant to be a wonderful starry occasion for a girl, or so the rubbishy books and magazines which we devoured told us.

I wore my cousin's evening dress and I had a month without sleep in case she would tell anyone of her charity. Generous as the gift was, it was not generously fitting enough and I had to have a huge panel of blue velvet let into each side. There was a fashion then for diamanté ear-rings, and I wore them so often rehearsing for the big night that I developed two great sores on my ears and I had to put sticking plaster on my lobes. Because I thought the plaster looked a bit less than lovely I painted it, and it ran, and lines of blue ran down my neck.

Perhaps it was that that made nobody want to dance with me. Maybe it was the two bits of velvet in my dress, it *could* have been the glazed insincere smile on my face. Anyway, whatever it was, there I sat, for four hours and forty-three minutes excluding supper, where nobody talked to me. When I came home I told my parents that I had a marvellous time, that my feet were sore from dancing and that it was lovely to be a grown-up at last. They were pleased at my success and they went to bed happy. I went to my room and tore the bits of blue sticking plaster off my ears and cried all night because I thought that in a hundred homes people were telling their parents that nobody had danced with me.

What I really wanted I never knew in those days, because I was too busy finding out what the acceptable thing to be was, and then trying to be it. I don't know where I developed all these extraordinary notions about having to compete, because I grew up in a very happy secure family who had no wish to push me into any other kind of world except the one we all lived in apparently contentedly. There was no social climbing, no keeping up with the Murphys. Yet I had managed to convince myself that I was on some kind of public treadmill and that everybody was looking at me to see whether or not I would fall off.

Looking back on it, I see that so much of it was utter fantasy, yet it seemed very real to me at the time. Why else would I have equipped myself with a library of books about things like how to eat oysters correctly, and how to address a duke in speech and on an envelope or what to do if invited to a country house for a weekend and how to speak to the butler? I don't know any dukes or butlers or country houses or oysters for heaven's sake, yet I felt that I must be prepared to cope with them when they came along so that I could marry someone of enormous wealth and standing.

In the middle of this fantasy I was constantly wondering what the people living around me thought of me and what kind of impression I was making on them. I thought because I was fat I had to try harder and in my still regular chats with this friendly easy-going Irish God, I would tell him that I supposed that being fat was one of the trials and tribulations that he gave to all those who were going to be numbered amongst his saint persons. And since God didn't actually deny it, I assumed that I had got it right.

One day I was sitting in a park near the university, worrying as usual whether I would look foolish sitting there by myself if any of my friends passed by: worrying in case my anorak was too shiny and new and whether I should roll it in the grass to make it look scruffy and more like everyone else's, when I read a passage from a French essay that we had to study that week. It wasn't very revolutionary, I suppose, but it changed my life. There was a line about a woman who was always wishing away the present in anticipation of the future, just like I was always doing. Apparently the woman spent most of her waking hours trying to impress people, and hardly any time actually living her life. It was as if the letters of the sentence had been written in fire. Now most people grow up gradually, or mature slowly or learn by experience or do things in some reasonable kind of progression, but I do everything suddenly. That very moment, I realised as if I had had a vision that my whole twenty years had been spent running a futile race, I could now get off this idiotic circuit and be myself. It didn't matter if I was sitting in this park by myself for ten years, nobody would notice, nobody would care. In fact it didn't matter what I did, nobody was watching me.

I suddenly knew now that the next time I went into a shop and an assistant curled up her lip and said: 'In *your* size Madam. . . . Oh no, I don't think we would have anything like that . . .' that it wasn't the end of the world, it just meant that the shop was inadequately stocked, and that they had therefore lost the sale of a dress by their inefficiency. If, in fact, I succeeded in the strange race we were all running and suppose for one mad moment that I actually won – that I became beautiful and charming and poised and married a successful wealthy man, would people love me and admire me? Not at all, they would hate me because they would be jealous. So it was all a game where the rules were bent and the dice was loaded against the player. You couldn't win.

It was as if someone had lifted a huge load from my chest, I felt lighter and freer than I ever remembered having felt. I suppose to anyone who might have been looking at me on that park bench I might have appeared the same but inside I was totally different. And I also knew it wasn't a mood that was going to disappear, it was no false elation, it was a gift. And just because I didn't care at all about them, all the things that I had wanted so desperately came my way. Long before women's lib I had liberated myself. The things that I felt able to do then, like going into a pub and having a pint by myself, don't seem brave now, but they were then because nobody else was doing them. To travel alone in those days looked foolhardy and pathetic, but I did it happily because I wasn't trying to be foolhardy and I now knew I wasn't pathetic. It was a joyful liberation because it touched so many things. For instance today if I sit in a car and the seat-belts won't reach around me, I just ask how do you make them bigger.

It now makes me very angry when I see people trying to perpetuate the myth that clouded my youth. I feel nothing but rage about those who tell the young, the weak, the defenceless, the inadequate, that they buy their way into a new and happier world. I think that this is against the trade descriptions act of any land, because you do *not* become happier, more self-confident, more secure if you paint your nails what somebody tells you is the right shade of red or buy a fur coat you can't afford and learn painfully how to dress clothes around you in what someone has called an elegant manner. You will have become enmeshed in a spiral of insecurity because you will now be worrying about the next level, the next achievement. What you should be told is that nobody gives a damn.

If I could share anything with anyone it would be that moment all those years ago in the park, the experience that divided the real from the artificial, the day that taught me what was real tragedy and what was only idiotic, manipulated nonsense. I have a gift which is far greater than beauty and fame and success. I have done terrible things which turned out not to be terrible at all because of this wonderful knowledge that only I would have thought them terrible in the first place. It is not a hundred per cent effective this magic transformation, sometimes I feel inadequate still. I feel too fat, too dull, too ill-informed, too shy. But I only have to remind myself that nobody is watching me, and then it's all fine again. If I had spent a life-time reading etiquette books, teach-yourself manuals, attending courses on grace and poise, following fashion magazines slavishly, trying method after method of getting slim I couldn't have bought such confidence and such happiness as the entirely unexpected happening that cost nothing and changed my life.

GAIL MAGRUDER
BEHIND THE HEADLINES

Until recently everything about our lives had been 'right'. To some people we were like a storybook couple – the handsome man and the pretty lady who got married and lived happily ever after – and I think we believed that about ourselves. Even our children were 'right'. When they were tiny they were never too fat or too thin. They were beautiful and healthy and full of humour. Everything we did turned out well. Jeb always had an exciting job. We had a lovely home and we made friends easily. Bad things just didn't happen to us. With all the travelling we did, there never was an accident, hardly even a close call. We seldom were sick. People used to tell us we brightened their day. We were nominal Christians, but we didn't need God. But that was before Watergate.

I suppose for us it all started when my husband was invited to work as special assistant to the President at the White House. I should have been happy about it but I wasn't. I would have felt guilty if I'd stood in his way and though I really didn't want to leave our friends and family I agreed and four months later we were off to Washington. Our names were automatically put in the directory of important government officials and business leaders, which meant we were on the official party list. The formality and the pace of life threatened to overwhelm us from the moment we arrived. We were inundated with invitations, sometimes to as many as four parties a night. At first, my inclination was to back away from so many after-hours activities. But I didn't want to be like most wives of White House staff, waving goodbye to my husband at 7 am and not seeing him again until late at night, I had to go along with him.

I really enjoy my children and try to be with them as much as I can. But I found myself having to choose between them and my husband when it came to evening hours and weekends. It was a difficult decision to make, but I made it in favour of Jeb. The long hours he worked eventually would strain his relationship with the children and me. If I holed up at home, soon there might not be any relationship at all. But if I went with him to as many functions as I could squeeze in, I might be some sort of a bridge between him and the children.

I realised that this was no ordinary job my husband had. He was working near the nerve centre of the most vital office in the world, dealing with problems that affected the lives of millions of people not only at home but in other countries. I had expected our new life to be demanding, but I was not prepared for its possessiveness. At times it seemed to me that Jeb was not supposed to have any private life at all.

For me, Watergate began long before the actual break-in. Six months before Jeb had told me about Gordon Liddy's suggestions, which included such things as prostitutes, blackmail and kidnapping. I was sick with disgust. Is this what men close to the President spent their time talking about! I couldn't believe it. My reaction startled Jeb. He was so caught up in Nixon's mania to get information that I don't think he ever gave a thought to the fact that such activities were illegal. I knew it was standard procedure in political campaigns for each side to spy on the other side, but this was evil.

It was in June of 1972 that I began to fear that there wouldn't be any 'normal' for us again. We were in California, at the Beverley Hills Hotel, when Gordon Liddy telephoned Jeb and told him that James McCord and the others had been caught trying to break into the Democratic campaign headquarters at the Watergate. It was a dizzying weekend and I was not aware of what was happening. Jeb succeeded in keeping it from me, which wasn't hard to do, considering all the commotion around us.

Jeb had always been an outgoing, gregarious, relating person.

Now he was becoming moody and introspective. I didn't know it then but the extent of his involvement with something illegal was getting through to him. And at the very moment that he was beginning to face the truth about what he and the others had done, he was joining in their attempt to cover up their guilt with lies. He was irritable with me and the children. I was miserable, but, more than my own pain, I felt the pain of our children, who couldn't understand why daddy rebuffed them when they tried to jump on his lap or roughhouse with him.

Jeb had always worked well under pressure – he was that kind of person who not only created it but could take it. The campaign was going so well and the re-election of Richard Nixon seemed assured, why was he cracking? I was beginning to gather up the pieces of the picture, but I was reluctant to put them together. I was afraid of what I might see. Richard Nixon was re-elected, and almost immediately we were caught up in plans for the inauguration, which Jeb was appointed to manage.

In June, August and September of 1972, Jeb was called to testify before a grand jury investigating the CREEP campaign. Two of those times he perjured himself. Our relationship was so damaged by that time that we couldn't even discuss the accusations that were being made. Communication was zero. I can't say that I suspected Jeb of being involved in anything illegal. I don't think I was able to face that possibility squarely. But certain things troubled me and made me doubt. Each time Jeb had to go before the grand jury, he had been extremely nervous, which wasn't like him. Speaking before a group of any size had never bothered him before. Why was he so worried about appearing before twenty-seven men and women? On the nights before he had to testify he couldn't sleep. He kept getting up and going to the living room so he wouldn't keep me awake with his restlessness.

Yes, I knew something was wrong. The jury believed Jeb, but that didn't make me feel any better. He was too defensive. He was drinking more and drinking faster. I couldn't believe that I was actually grateful he was seldom home with the children. I didn't want them to see him that way, and I knew that I could not live much longer with a man who was as alienated from me as Jeb was.

At last I put the pieces together. My husband was involved in illegal activities and would have to pay for what he had done. And at the beginning of April Jeb decided to go to the prosecutors and tell them the truth. The first day Jeb met with the prosecutors he was gone for a long time. When he came home, I was startled by the look on his face. He was tired, but he was smiling just a little. For the first time in months, he was relaxed. He didn't want a drink. He seemed happy to see me. Although he would never be the same, he was at last recognisable as the man I had loved and married and still loved very deeply. We put our arms around each other, I had my husband back and at that moment it mattered more than anything else in the world.

While Jeb was working with the prosecutors almost daily for sixteen months he was out of work so we had no income. And all the time we were worried about what the sentence might be. In January he went to the judge and asked to be sentenced so that he could get it over with as soon as possible. Finally, in May, he went to court. As Jeb and his lawyers stood to receive the sentence, I held onto my pastor's hand so hard that I knew my fingernails were digging into him. I remember thinking how I must be hurting him, but there was nothing I could do to loosen my grip. He didn't move. He just let me hold onto him. I had a strange sense of being outside myself watching what was going on. I heard the words, 'Ten months to four years in prison', and I was afraid I would either faint or become hysterical. I did neither. In fact I felt strangely calm, almost numb. It was a form of shock. I realise now that it was this form of shock that was God's way of protecting me.

Someone took my arm and guided me toward Jeb. The same thing had happened to him. He looked the way he did always, except for his eyes. We heard familiar voices and when we turned toward the spectators' seats in the courtroom we saw the faces of friends and neighbours. We hadn't expected that. Later, much later, when we could begin to feel again, we would be grateful for their love. We knew it was one of God's ways of sustaining us. It was a stiff sentence. Everything was drowned out by the awful scream inside of me that no one else could hear. 'Oh God! Dear God! Help us!' My inner scream went on and on. But outwardly I maintained a façade of calm. We went to our son's graduation where he was honoured for academic achievement and we sat there surrounded by Washington political officials who knew I would be taking Jeb to prison on Tuesday.

The children and I went to see Jeb each weekend. When I asked for Jeb I had to ask for him by number. While the prison official called his number over the intercom they searched me and my children. We were very frightened. I had been told that our first visit would be the crucial one, because a man who goes to prison is afraid his wife and children will reject him. Our behaviour would be very important. I had no way of knowing how our children would react to seeing Jeb as I had seen him. Each one was so different. Whitney was fourteen and very responsible. I knew he wouldn't want to cry. Justin at twelve was realising that he wasn't a child any more. His deep feelings would be hard for him to handle. Tracy, at ten, was beginning to take after me. She kept her feelings to herself, but I knew they were there. And little Stuart was seven. He had a special need for Jeb because he was just too young to understand why his father didn't come home any more.

The first thing I noticed about Jeb when I saw him was that he was perspiring heavily, which was very unusual for him. His face was wet. He was pale and his eyes were glazed. He came towards us stiffly, slowly, as if he were made of wood. Fortunately the children didn't wait. As soon as he was past the guard, they threw themselves at him, hugging and kissing him and talking all at once. I felt their need for him and I smiled, seeing them together. But Jeb didn't respond. He couldn't smile or laugh or say a word. He just stood there, letting the children cling to him. His feelings were so strong that I think he was afraid of breaking down in front of us.

We felt as if we would choke because our hearts were so filled with love. Our prayers came so easily. There was no self-consciousness about them, no wondering whether they were acceptable to God. He was right there with us and we could feel his love. It was the most joyous experience I have ever known. But for a person who is sent to prison, the sentence never ends. We were together again as a family but we were not the same. In some ways, the period immediately after Jeb's release was the hardest time of all. It was almost as if we were recovering from the death of someone close to us. Actually the child in both of us had died. The cruel but simple fact is that once a man has been dehumanised, he can't become human again overnight.

I am different too. I don't know whether I have become stronger or simply realised my strength, but I am not the same kind of wife. I want to share in the decision making, and there has to be something of me in our goals. And here are some things I wish now for my family: I hope we can be close together in the few years that are left before our children go off to build lives of their own. I hope our children will not be scarred by the traumatic events in our lives. I hope my husband and I can do productive, creative work that will be of value to others. We pray for our friends in prison. Each one of them a child of God just as I am. These men are my brothers and they are hurting. I pray that my children, my husband and I will continue to grow in the Lord.

U p until the time I went to Chile I was a very ordinary sort of doctor, very concerned with the rat-race, wanting to be successful, not so much to be rich, but wanting to be very good at my work and have a nice house and a car and do all the things I like doing. I chose Chile because I had some Chilean friends and they told me it was a very beautiful country and it sounded very attractive. I somehow visualised myself as working shorter hours and living the grand life and probably marrying some tall, gorgeous, handsome man, so I set off to seek my fortune. I would like to be very clear that I didn't go out to look for and serve the poor. I went out as a private person, perhaps escaping from the hardness of medical life in England. And for a while it looked as if my dream would be true.

I gradually grew to see, however, the other side of Chile. With the worsening of the country's economic situation hospitals began to change and the poor and unemployed no longer had the right to free medical treatment. I started working for a church clinic in the shanty-towns and then for the first time I came face to face with the reality of poverty and suffering and hunger. In the shanty-towns I was working with priests and nuns and this led to my being asked to treat the wounded revolutionary which resulted in my being arrested. I was asked to treat a wounded man who was unable to go to hospital because the police were after him. I treated him just as a doctor would without really thinking a lot about it, and then suddenly I found myself in prison.

For the first twenty-four hours in prison I was interrogated and subjected to a lot of physical pain. People threatened to kill me and I thought that perhaps I was going to die. So for the first time l suddenly thought perhaps this is the end of my life. From having said in a blasé sort of way before: 'Of course I don't mind dying, it'll all be okay,' I suddenly thought: 'Is it all true, does God exist, am I making a frightful mistake, is it all a fairy story?' But I just hung on to everything that I remembered and I came to the conclusion that it was all true. But I didn't feel warm and comforted by this because it was just a cold-blooded, intellectual decision.

Prayer has always been important to me and during the year before I was imprisoned I had disciplined myself to pray regularly every day and in many situations. During the actual time of torture, I prayed in a very desperate way, a sort of 'Help me God' kind of prayer. It seemed it was the only thing to do, a matter of praying for strength to hold on because all the time they were torturing me, they were trying to make me give away the names of people who I thought at that time they were going to take and kill. So I was very desperate not to give in and I just prayed: 'Oh God, help me, help me'.

It wasn't a particularly comforting sort of prayer, it was just a very anguished cry in the dark. What was comforting was that I suddenly felt enormously close to him, because I realised that I had in a way perhaps participated in his suffering. I suppose it was a sort of Calvary experience. It seems proud to say that but it wasn't meant that way. I tried to express what I felt on paper. To be stripped of my clothes and stretched out in such a defence-less way made me dare to think that perhaps I was experiencing in some slight way what Christ had suffered. All during that hard, very dark time I just felt that he was there and I asked him to help me to hang on. And it was then that I understood the truth of St Paul when he said, 'Nothing can separate us from the love of Christ – not nakedness, nor peril, nor sword'.

What I found curious, even at that time, was that I felt no hatred for the people who were torturing me. I just felt sorry for them and I could see how Christ forgave the people who tortured him, because it was so obvious they were such sad, sick people. After four days of physical pain, I was moved into a new world and with it a new set of problems. I was left completely alone in a small room with just a bed, and half of the Bible in Spanish, an old *Reader's Digest* and a tiny glimpse of the mountains over a high brick wall. I was filled with an enormous amount of fear that I had to keep very tightly battened down, because it was quite possible that any moment in that time they could have taken me back and tortured me again, or they could have killed me. On a more practical level there was the problem of actually spending twenty-four hours a day alone. I had to organise myself physically and emotionally to cope with this length of time. And if you are very frightened and you don't know what's going to happen it's that much more difficult. I think it's the same perhaps for people who live alone, who are ill and perhaps afraid of dying. I tried very hard to think just what God wanted of me at this time. And I remembered vividly the prayer of Dietrich Bonhoeffer written while he was awaiting execution in a Nazi prisoner of war camp.

O God, early in the morning I cry to you.
Help me to pray
And to concentrate my thoughts on you;
I cannot do this alone.

In me there is darkness,
But with you there is light;
I am lonely, but you do not leave me;
I am feeble in heart, but with you there is help;
I am restless, but with you there is peace.
In me there is bitterness, but with you there is patience;
I do not understand your ways,
But you know the way for me.

Restore me to liberty,
And enable me so to live now
That I may answer before you and before men.
Lord, whatever this day may bring,
Your name be praised.
Amen.

So I tried very hard not to fight against what God wanted for me and this is why I fought against the desire to pray to be released. I prayed endlessly that God should do what he wanted, that if I was to die, then so be it. But I prayed that I should have the strength to die decently and with dignity. One of the most difficult times was the night after my first visit to the judge, where I had to face for the first time that perhaps I wasn't going to be released and that maybe I was going to spend five or maybe ten years in jail. This was a terrible night. I felt very near to breaking, and I prayed as did the soldier in the trench under fire in Gerald Kersh's *The Soldier:*

Stay with me God, the night is dark –
the night is cold, my little spark
of courage dies. The night is long;
Be with me God, and make me strong.
Life with its change of mood and shade
I want to live. I'm not afraid,
But me and mine are hard to part,
Oh, unknown God, lift up my heart.

I lay awake all night fighting with my natural urge to pray to be saved and released. This trying to abandon myself to the will of God was much harder than the experience of torture. Torture was imposed on me whereas abandonment is a voluntary act.

I prayed for strength, I prayed to know what was right, I tried to love Him, praise Him, thank Him. There was a lot to thank Him for. I thanked Him for the fact that I had a bed, that I had enough to eat, that I was alive, that I was well, that I had a book, a million different things. I thanked him for the birds that came and ate the crumbs on the windowsill and for the grass and for the little bit of the mountains that I could see. Then I used to pray for other people. I prayed for all the other people who had been tortured and who were being tortured, I prayed that they should have strength.

After three weeks alone, I was forced into yet another totally different situation. I was moved to a detention camp where there were 120 other women. We slept eight to a room in tiered bunks, two people sleeping on the floor and so one was just never alone. Suddenly, instead of thinking perhaps very much about myself all day, I had to think much more about my relationship with other people and to try to see how I should behave to help them. After having been alone for so long I was quite overwhelmed by their love and generosity. They worried desperately if they thought I was unwell or depressed. I came to realise that they loved me specially because I, who was not a Marxist, had helped one of them. They showered gifts upon me, all the more precious because they made them specially for me and they gave me things that were of special significance to them. They gave me a cross made out of matchsticks and wool, and beads made out of bread by a girl who spent many weeks in solitary confinement. A very special gift of miniature chalices made out of coins was sent to me from the men's section of the prison, and a Bible, given to me by the Red Cross in Chile, was signed by many of my friends in prison the day I left.

The women prisoners were all young and professional like myself and many of them were unbelievers. I was known to be a Catholic, so that when the first Sunday came, people said to me: 'Are you going to hold a service?'. I had never held a service in my life and I was extremely embarrassed about it, and so very diffidently, I put up a little notice that said: 'Anybody who wants to pray, we'll do it outside.' I was ashamed at how much it cost me to make this public witness, but to my great surprise, about twenty-five people came. We sat down on the grass with a cross in the middle, and I tried to pick bits out of the Bible which would comfort people and help them. We prayed spontaneously. We prayed for the husbands, the families, the lovers, the people who were lost and the children. I tried to share the thoughts that I had at that time. One of the things that came to me very strongly was the meaning of liberty. I translated Richard Lovelace's beautiful poem, *To Althea from Prison*, for the prisoners and later I wrote it out and gave it to the friends who came to visit me to explain to them how I felt:

Stone walls do not a prison make,
Nor iron bars a cage;
Minds innocent and quiet take
That for an hermitage;
If I have freedom in my love
And in my soul am free,
Angels alone, that soar above,
Enjoy such liberty.

We talked about this poem a lot in prison and came to the conclusion that the freedom of the spirit that we had was a very real thing and although we were surrounded by ten-foot walls, barbed wire and chaps with machine guns, that really we were quite free. It was the people who held us prisoner who were enslaved. The torturers were prisoners of some unspeakable evil, perhaps the rich people who were unable to share their goods with people who didn't have enough to eat were also slaves of their own property. And we prayed for progressive freedom for ourselves, from our own selfishness.

Since I came back from Chile so many people have asked me if praying helped me while I was in prison. I have no doubt that it was of enormous help to me, especially during my time in solitary confinement. And I think the fact that prayer had become such an integral part of my life before I became a prisoner made it possible for me to face the unknown with a calm that surprised even myself.

In April 1976 I made the decision to become a nun. This was the culmination of twenty years running away from God. I had felt called to give myself to God in a very total sort of way ever since I was at school. But I had been unable to face the loss of my liberty as I then saw it. With the making of this decision, however, there came an immense peace and strength. This decision had involved the writing as it were of a blank cheque to God. It was a very difficult thing to do, but having done it, everything that followed I just naturally accepted as being part of his plan for me. Although I was frightened and anguished, in my heart I was at peace, because I knew that he was driving and not me.

Working backwards if one is to arrive at the point of letting God take over the wheel you have to come to know him very closely and so to trust him utterly. One can get to know God in many ways but especially through prayer. This is something which anybody can do anywhere. To me prayer is talking to God. I can tell him how I'm feeling if I'm feeling miserable, I tell him so and if I'm feeling happy and joyful I can thank him for that. I tell him if I want something desperately or if I'm desperately worried about something. It is essentially an act of the will. I choose to raise my mind and heart to God, to love him, to praise him, to thank him and to ask him for what I want. I find that the more I come to know God through quiet formal prayer in church the more I find him everywhere, in people and in nature. For me the world is truly charged with the grandeur of God.

I have found by bitter experience that prayer time can so easily be squeezed out of my day by all the good that I fancy I am doing. So I have learned to discipline myself to pray each day and in every possible situation. Personally I find it easiest to pray in a beautiful church or in places of great natural beauty and I find it difficult to be peaceful in my room. Struggling with this problem, I have learned to use darkness as a means of pushing aside the cares of the day and to be alone with God. It is possible to create from a perfectly ordinary bedroom a setting where it is quite easy to pray. With just an ordinary candle and a box of matches I have my own portable church. So, sitting on the floor, looking at my candle, I sit with him as I would sit with a friend, sometimes talking, sometimes listening and sometimes just being there. It may be that I am tired, and fed up so I tell him: 'Lord, I am miserable and I want to go back to bed, please accept this muddled sort of prayer and help me to face today and not be too bad-tempered and selfish, in fact just Lord help'.

I have found that this faithfulness to formal prayer in this way has had an enormous pay off in terms of joy and peace and ability to cope with my life. I find God more and more in the ordinary things and the people round me. As I walk in a crowd or sit in a bus he is with me, sometimes present as Christ in the people around me and sometimes as my all powerful and almighty God. This almost perpetual sensation of the presence of God in my life has added an almost unbelievable dimention of joy and radiance to my life. So that I now understand how it is that the men signed with the cross of Christ go gaily in the dark.

ANNE BANCROFT
A CROWNING CLARITY

When I was young I lived in the country. Trees and wind and grass mattered very much to me, especially the wind. When the branches of the great beech trees were swaying, or when clouds were blown across the moon, or when the wind was soft and moved through long grass, I felt sure that there was a wonder and a mystery and all the world was somehow full of a meaning which I couldn't really understand and couldn't reach. But I desperately wanted to know the heart of that meaning and I had an intense longing to break through and to enter that marvellous world of light and wind and movement, to be one with it. I was sure that I truly belonged to it and that it had a great deal to do with God, whom I called the Presence because he seemed often to be present to me when I was alone in the fields and woods.

But when I was sixteen I became afraid and stopped it all. I was afraid that I might lose myself altogether and although I had wanted this when I was younger, now the outer, everyday world had attractions for me too and I began to reject the inner, solitary quest.

When I was still very young I married and started a family. The years began to trickle past but the marriage was not a happy one, we were completely unsuited to each other, and it ended with a bitter sense of guilt and failure. I kept the children and took them to America, where I remarried. But this marriage too was founded on sand and not on rock and in a last-ditch effort to keep it going I persuaded my husband to return with us to England, hoping that a calmer and saner society might help us both. I think it did, but it was too late to save the relationship.

It was when this marriage too seemed doomed to end in a wasteland of quarrels, jealousy, fear and hatred, that I suddenly woke up to the fact that something had gone badly wrong, not just with this situation but with me. Looking hard at myself I saw that I had become really futile, so much a slave to my emotions, so involved with my own feelings, so centred on myself that my life had narrowed down to the compulsive behaviour of a zombie. Where was the true I? I saw clearly that something vital was missing in me. It lay there out of my reach, even beyond my imagination, because I could not see what it was; I only knew I was without it.

I then came to a time of great despair. In the middle of ordinary life – of looking after my children and sending them to school and playing with them, trying not to be inadequate for them – I saw myself as a person of no light, a person who was thick, opaque and joyless, not a real person at all. A tremendous sense of remorse came over me for the years I had messed up so badly, and an enormous depression closed down on me because I thought I would now never discover any world of the spirit, just as I had never quite reached it in my childhood, although now I was even further away.

One night I could not go to bed and I sat still all night, feeling a great repentance and sadness of mind. When the morning light came and the birds began to sing, I suddenly found myself strangely aware of them. I looked into the garden and saw a blackbird and it was as though I had never seen a blackbird before. It had a significance which was completely new to me and I suddenly felt that this blackbird was the most real thing I had ever seen, and that just to see a blackbird in this way would make life worth living. The days that followed were different from any that had passed before. I was suddenly intensely aware of sound and light and found myself more vulnerable than usual to the impact of other people. Other things – a group of trees – would fleetingly take on the significance of the blackbird. I realised I was coming close to something, some new quality.

One evening I was looking at a branch of rhododendron

which I had put in a vase. As I looked, enjoying its beauty but without any purpose in my mind, I suddenly felt a sense of communication with it, as though it and I had become one. It seemed to come from my forehead and the feeling was immeasurably happy and strong. It came to me then that the whole mystery of existence – that mystery which I was so aware of in my childhood – was not far away from me but very close at hand. And that somehow the secret lay in my relationship with everything about me. That strange sense of oneness with the rhododendron seemed to have come about because I was still, and not wanting anything, and therefore somehow free to see it properly and to know it as itself.

I wished I could know everything in this way and then I found myself thinking, why not? It was only myself that was stopping me. There was no limit to the amount of love that I could give to anything I saw. And then I realised that for most of my life I had never done this. I had thought lots of things not worth my attention because they gave me nothing in return. But now I could not imagine how I could have spent so long turning away from things or being indifferent to them. No wonder I had never kept the love of husband or lover; I had never loved properly myself. But now I would be able to reach out to people and everyday life. Without barriers I would always be able to gaze and listen, not just to clouds and trees, but to all life. I felt a great sense of peace and proportion, as though an obsession had left me and I was myself again.

A few days later a new and somehow crowning experience came. It was in the morning and I switched on the wireless to hear a concert. As the first note of music sounded, there was an almost audible click in my mind and I found that everything was transformed. I was in a different state of consciousness altogether. It was as though the separate feeling of 'me' which we all feel had gone, clicked away, and instead there was a great sense of clarity, of utter beneficent, wonderful emptiness. And in that emptiness there were no barriers. The stones on the road were exquisitely beautiful and as significant as a person. An upright, old-fashioned bicycle propped up by the road was wonderfully funny. It was as though my mind could now embrace, without reserve, all that it encountered whether people or animals or things, because it was living in clearness and emptiness. I was in this state of the completest and greatest happiness for three days. I thought it would last all my life and was desolate when it faded and went.

After it had gone, I decided I must investigate a path quite new to me, which was that of religion. It seemed to me that what had happened must be, in its own way, a spiritual experience, although I had never read or heard of anything quite like it. But the effect of that crowning clarity and of those strange weeks of effort and discovery, made me utterly convinced that an unimaginable wonder exists as the essential beingness of everything. And that it exists whether I notice it or not, and that when I *do* notice it, as I did then, it transforms me. So I knew I could not forget it. I felt somehow as though I was turned round in my mind towards a different direction.

But there was no one I could talk to about this. So I tried to get the sort of book that might tell me something and I read a book by Aldous Huxley called *The Perennial Philosophy*. In this book he takes all the big things in life, such as love and pain and loneliness, and relates them to the various religions with quotations. And when I read the Buddhist quotations I felt immediately that my own experience fitted with Buddhism.

'With the light of words and understanding one must go beyond words and understanding and enter upon the path of realisation.' 'Nirvana is where there is no birth and no extinction; it is seeing into the state of suchness, absolutely transcending all the categories constructed by the mind.' 'Not by the slothful, nor by the fool, nor by the undiscerning, is that Nirvana to be reached which is the untying of all knots.'

The Buddha's teaching was wholly concerned with untying the knots in men's minds so that they can be open to reality and free from the greed and ignorance which bind them like chains. I discovered, through meditation, that seeing things in their suchness – the word Buddhists use for the essential nature of all things – seeing them as I once did without any barrier of 'me' to get in the way, was one of the great aims of Buddhism. This was a big relief to me because I didn't want pious talk or a guilty feeling that I should attend some sort of church. I wanted, and found, a straightforward acceptance that man's deepest need is not to live by bread alone but to transcend all his thoughts and feelings and to *know* the meaning of timeless reality, and of God.

I found that a Chinese Zen monk, Hui Neng, had once described that marvellous emptiness of the mind and that he could teach me how to reach it again. 'As in the outer world, we can see that space contains the sun and the moon and the stars, so true awakening is to realise that the essence of mind is empty like space, in which thoughts come and go.' His teaching was that instead of trying to purify one's ordinary mind, one must simply let go of it by letting go of the thoughts and impressions which come into it, neither repressing them nor holding onto them nor interfering with them; above all it means letting go of *ideas* and not letting them have power over one. For basic unhappiness, said the Buddha, is really caused by thinking of ourselves each as a separate, isolated individual, alone in the world and bound some day to die. But when we can transcend that idea and when we can understand that the real basis of our life is not this small, finite individuality, but is the mysterious and infinite suchness of existence, the nature of God, then our worst suffering may come to an end.

Most people ask me, 'Are you a Buddhist?' And I usually say yes, because in many ways I am a Buddhist, in that I have found the Buddha's teaching immeasurably helpful, understanding, compassionate and wise. But in my heart of hearts I think I remain uncommitted to any 'ism' or religion, because I know that the truth and the splendour transcends them all.

VERA VON DER HEYDT
A JOURNEY

I was brought up with fairy tales and folk tales and myths of all descriptions. Many of the myths frightened me when I was a little girl, because of the jealousies and fights between the Gods, but fairy tales did not affect me in the same way. They were more homely and I found it easier to identify with the main characters particularly when I realised there was bound to be a happy ending. I loved the stories in which the hero had to leave home and go far away to find a treasure which might be gold, or a golden fleece, a blue flower or a miraculous cup. It was always difficult to attain and great dangers had to be overcome before it was found. The heroes were invariably good and beautiful. They were usually compassionate, willing to work and open-hearted. But they had to learn about evil and ugliness. Very rarely did they have to brave the mortal dangers on their paths unaided. Helpful creatures, animals, human beings, even gods, appeared at the right time, helping, advising and guiding those who were prepared to accept help.

In the *Frog Prince*, for instance, the Princess throws the horrid, disgusting frog against the wall when he molests her and lo, he is turned into a beautiful Prince. This was important to me, for the Princess disobeyed, just as I had always wished to be able to disobey. In the Frau Holle story, a girl serves her faithfully, without thinking of herself and she is rewarded by a strange gift. Every time she speaks, gold drops from her lips. Since it was impressed on me that people always had ulterior motives it was good to know that this was not altogether true. I have always cried when I read the story of the little mermaid who becomes human and acquires a soul when she dies for the love of the

Prince. It dawned on me then that suffering and sacrifice and even death is connected with love. Of the myths, Amor and Psyche particularly fascinated me partly because of the wonderful help Psyche got in fulfilling her task to regain her lover but most of all because in the end she actually fails and yet in this failure is her ultimate triumph. I learned that one may fail.

Suddenly I knew that I too was on a journey, on a quest, but I did not know what for and I did not know where to. Looking back as I do now, I do not see things in chronological order. This journey of mine has taken on a dream-like quality, and I see the past in a sequence of meaning rather than of time. There was the outer journey which took me away from Berlin and Germany to Britain. But the journey I am talking about now is the inner one and like all journeys it has a beginning and many milestones on the way, but unlike the outer journey it has no end. I never felt heroic and I did not know what I was looking for. I waited and I protected myself with a shell of convention whilst wondering and listening behind it.

In fact I suppose this need to separate from my parents and my background was probably one of the first stages of my journey. I also found helpers on the way, people, books, like Goethe's *Wilhelm Meister* and more indirectly all the arts. The first picture that got through to me was a landscape by Cézanne. I could dream myself into this landscape and explore the mountains which were near and yet so far away. I saw the painting at a dealers. I wanted it terribly badly, the first thing I really wanted to own. I could have bought it for 100 marks (£5) but I did not have the money and I did not want to ask my parents for it. In a different way a painting of daffodils, by a friend of mine, epitomised for me the feeling of spring and of Easter – the Resurrection.

I only saw sculptures by Marino Marini comparatively recently, yet his riders and horses so intimately united, expressing wonder and power, joy and despair, reminded me most vividly of an Arab horse I once owned and which played an important role in my imagination when I was trying to solve a difficult problem in my life. In my mind I was riding, knowing that I had to jump an obstacle. My horse refused to jump. In spite of everything I did to try and coax it across. Finally one night before going to sleep I decided to throw away the reins although it frightened me to do so. When I woke up in the morning I knew that the horse had jumped. I also knew that it was I who had refused to jump and at the same time it was me who did wish to continue the journey. I stayed in my shell for quite a long time, but it was broken when my marriage disintegrated and it was shattered by Hitler.

We lived in Berlin. My father was Jewish, my mother was not, so I had to come out into the open with my attitudes to what was happening. I was always frightened of endangering my family, so I left Germany and started my new life in London. Probably as a result of being more on my own, things came to the surface which I had thought about a great deal without doing anything about them. One night I dreamed, yet I was half awake, and I saw a statue of the Sacred Heart come alive and I heard Christ calling me three times. This happened three nights running. I followed the call as I understood it and I joined the Roman Catholic Church. This was the beginning of an intensified journey – it was by no means the end of it. During the war I went to Oxford and there I met my first analyst, a very brilliant intuitive man who started me on the path of being an analyst myself. I felt happy and privileged when I was asked to join a clinic in Edinburgh. I should have been satisfied by then, but I wasn't. I knew that I was going round and round in a circle like an old circus horse.

Suddenly I decided that I had to get out of it and that I was going to spend a holiday in Switzerland, in Ascona, a lovely place I remembered well from former times. There I met Carl Jung who encouraged me to go to Zurich for a while and he suggested that I should visit him regularly if I could arrange a sabbatical. I could do this, and one day I found myself sitting with Jung for the first time in his consulting room. Something quite unexpected happened to me then. Jung spoke to me in

German as a matter of course, but I had not noticed it in Ascona. It hit me when I told him dreams and experiences in German.

I had a strange experience very soon after I had come to Zurich. I had been sitting in a chapel by myself when I saw a priest coming into the sanctuary to say mass. Suddenly I realised that Christ himself was there and that he was offering me the bread and wine. There was not much to say about this experience before I myself had assimilated it and it was part of Jung's genius that he didn't make any comment, so I went on telling him dreams which I had had around that time. It was then that it dawned on me how cut off I had felt from my roots living in a British culture which knew so little about mine. Jung received amplifications and associations without my having to go into long explanations, because he knew the background and the context from which they sprang. When a black poodle appeared in my dreams he knew as well as I did that this was a reference to Mephistopheles, the devil, the spirit of negation in Goethe's *Faust*. Or else that a young man in my dream, who I called Carlos, stood for the human spirit of affirmation of life in spite of tyranny and death in Schiller's drama *Don Carlos*.

Words, whole sentences, quotations, all in my mother tongue, flooded back into my mind, and it was a revelation to realise how viciously I had slammed shut a door in distress and horror when I had left Germany. Jung gave me the key with which to re-open it. I rediscovered my own language and my own images. I understood that the words one uses to express one's feelings and thoughts, the words through which one experiences love and beauty for the first time become carriers, vehicles for the soul. My poor soul which had become atrophied and had shrivelled up due to my hate, came to life again; my spirit had always remained alive, but now my soul could sing again. I could continue my journey freer and more complete. There was no need to cover up anything any more in my second language, I could rejoice in it, and I could shed some of 'the mind-forged manacles' which had haunted me.

I still feel Zurich and Ascona to be 'Heimat', a kind of spiritual home, they were the places of re-birth and of initiation into the meaning of wholeness where inner and outer come together. Ascona was the place that my husband and I met again and were able to bury the unhappiness we had caused one another. It was there, too, that one of the foremost thinkers and Jewish mystics acknowledged me for what I was, in my totality. The split between my Jewish and my Aryan heritage was truly healed. I had come to a resting place, and very close to the treasure, but I knew that my journey was by no means at an end and that there was much that I still had to discover in myself which I would have to face in sorrow as well as in joy.

I returned to Scotland where people gave me so much in their directness and warmth. I still often think of the stark, lonely hills, the colour of the heather and the sea and the sky, the skirl of the pipes and their songs. Then I came back to London which has been my home for many years. In my dreams it has come to represent the centre of my being.

What about the journey now, what about the treasure, have I found it? I have learnt something; I now know that fairy tales can be misleading in their insistence on a happy ending. In myth the treasure may be found, but then it either leads to disaster or it is lost again. In life, the journey, the search, goes on. Every day is a new day, a new starting point; one finds, one loses; one knows and one does not know. Today is treasure – not yesterday, nor tomorrow, it is now – and change is treasure, and open doors, open eyes and an open heart. If we discover this, it is *Deo Concedente* – by the grace of God.

ERIN PIZZEY
KNOWING HOW IT FEELS

I work in the rougher side of life. I run refuges for battered women. There is violence and alcohol and a third of the men involved have done time for armed robbery. So sometimes rules get bent or we have to demonstrate and local housing authorities get annoyed. We are not dealing with tidy situations. This means sometimes we make news. But public protests and wrangles with the authorities aren't what the shelters are about.

We are dealing with personal lives – trying to give shelter to a woman, perhaps with children, who may be literally running for her life. People ask me what qualified help I have and my answer is 'my staff and my women'. They are qualified by their experience – they have all been through it and they have all begun to learn from it, and they know what someone needs who has just run from a violent house. And what qualifies me is that I'm the same as the others.

In my own case, the violence wasn't in my marriage, but in my home background. In my childhood, I was caught between two parents always fighting and quarrelling – my mother seemed to be the victim – and I became disturbed. I was sent away to boarding school and was punished for my lack of control and that made it worse. I was damaged and if you punish a damaged child all you do is push them further into being an outsider. It doesn't help to control them because there is no punishment you can hand out which is worse than what the child already remembers. Disturbed families lose their friends and so there was no one for me to turn to for help.

The final thing was that my mother died of cancer and my father was terribly distraught and fought with her all the time she was dying. When she died he didn't bury the body. For a whole week in summertime the body was in the house. He kept it in the dining room and made us look at it all the time. I went to the Vicar and I went to the doctor who knew us and no one would interfere. Four days after she died – she had decomposed quite a lot by then – my father called the doctor to check that my mother was dead. The doctor went into the dining room, looked at the corpse and came out and said 'It shouldn't happen to a dog'. Then he walked out and left us. Still no one to turn to.

Some years later, I started to become violent towards my own first child. I had never been mothered and we learn the maternal instinct from being taught it. If we aren't taught it, but come from a violent or unrestful family, the cry of a baby will often produce rage and not compassion. This is how I found myself reacting and that got me frightened. I went to a psychiatrist and I said 'I am frightened, I'm going to hurt my daughter.' And after talking to me for an hour, he said: 'Well the trouble is you're a bad mother' and I said 'I know, that's why I've come for help,' but he couldn't help. He had all the theories but he couldn't help me in the real life situation.

But fortunately for me it struck me that I was only a bad mother because I hadn't learned how to be a good one. As I began to come to terms with that, things improved. Now my daughter is fourteen years old and we have talked about all this a lot, because even if she doesn't remember it, it must be buried deep inside her. And now she understands me and my background. So I was lucky, I learned to mother through Cleo, my daughter, and by the time I had a son I was older and more mature. This sharing of experience by talking has turned out to be as important in my work since then as it was in my own family. Many of us have terrifically violent feelings towards our own children and feel guilty not realising that it is not so much that we are bad as that we are damaged – our own childhood left holes in us that may never ever be filled.

So that had been my background and I had become involved in running a community centre for young mothers and one day in came a woman called Kath. She took off her jersey and showed me her bruises. Kath had been married to a violent man for years, he had constantly beaten her up and she had finally run for it. She came through my door, saying no one would help her. And I knew exactly what she meant. She had been trapped and her children had been trapped and I knew how I'd been damaged and that violence always breeds more violence. So I knew she must have shelter and I took her in. By this time, her children were quite grown up. One daughter was married and had repeated the pattern by marrying a violent man, so it was Kath's daughter who was the next refugee. Then the word spread and it was like an explosion. One day there was no one and a few weeks later there were ten, twelve and it went on up.

I remember sitting up for two nights after taking Kath in a terrific state of rage and anger, that really nothing had changed. Kath had no one to turn to just as years before I hadn't. Since my childhood I suppose I had believed that things had improved and now I saw they hadn't.

Another thing I felt was a great faith that this was something that I could help with precisely because I knew how Kath felt. It is a very indescribable feeling because I'm a sort of child-like Christian. I don't go to church because I think the church isn't very relevant any more to what faith is about. But I always work on the principle that providing we follow the right path, and do the things we do with love, then everything will be all right.

So from this time on the shelter for battered wives just grew. And not long afterwards we moved to the house in Chiswick High Road where I spend most of my time. By this time there were fifty-six mothers and their kids. To an ordinary person who is in the middle of an ordinary marital quarrel, this place is a nightmare. But to the woman who is running for her life it's the safest place on earth and they just fall through the door.

Civil servants say to me 'But you can't just have an open door, what happens if you're overcrowded.' But to us it's perfectly simple, if someone needs refuge they get refuge. And there are advantages in numbers. I know from my own experience that if you live in a violent family you get used to a high adrenalin level. We need to work together. You can't take someone from an explosive family life and put them into a vacuum because the anxiety will drive them back to the violent situation. So I discovered in this great close-packed community that love and affection makes it a place where women will stay to get over their panic and begin to think rationally. They can talk things out with each other or with members of the staff.

Another advantage is that there isn't much privacy and that's a good thing. Every letter that comes to me or to the house I read out to everybody, and all the doors are open. There is no place to go and indulge in self pity. It's good because pain needs to come out into the open. It has always been kept so private that is why nothing gets done. When it is in the open it's amazing how much more bearable it gets.

The staff look after fund raising, general administration and housing details. We have got quite a few houses now. We run play groups for the children. The children are very important because if a child comes from a violent home they have got that violence in them and it takes time for them to begin to trust and grow again. The life we lead is pretty much a family life but it is multiplied by the number of families which means it changes into a sort of tribe. There is endless fixing and cleaning and mothering the children and plenty of problems to keep everyone busy. Sometimes there are explosions and that's OK because a house like this needs to blow off steam and so far we have always coped. If life hadn't prepared me for the kind of emotions and games that go on I wouldn't have been able to cope, but as it is I'm the biggest and most powerful woman in the house and if anybody wants to freak out they know I might come down and freak out much more.

For all of us it is a learning experience. We have women at our refuge who come from a terrible home, a prison, a mental hospital or wherever. They have always been labelled but here they find they are simply accepted. If they get terribly drunk they won't be locked up, someone will put them to bed. And if they do smash something – well it's not the end of the world. In fact they know they will still be loved and that's very healing. It's obvious to all of us that the openness of the experience is crucial – if we had little private offices where people crept away to talk about their shame, the shame stays with them.

Living in the middle of it I've certainly learned a lot about violence itself. There are two types of violence that I see. There is one kind that explodes immediately the person feels frustrated. Bang and out come the fists. That is quite an easy one to deal with, because I'm an explosive sort of person myself. There is another type of violence which is a bit more tricky. It may be a woman who seems meek and mild on the surface but within a few days she will have created conflict situations all round the house. For instance, we will all be doing something like cleaning up and she will just be sitting there. And sooner or later someone will say 'Why aren't you doing something' and she'll sit back and be a complete victim or she will cry and say 'Oh you're being horrid to me'. That is another kind of violence. But in a house like the refuge we do learn to see through each other's games terribly quickly. I have played all the games myself and I know what they are.

Another thing with violence, and this seems incredible, people get addicted to it. I remember a woman saying to one of the staff 'My husband is terribly violent, he's smashed the place up and beaten me up – but I must go back to get my clothes'. As one of the helpers put it 'Daniel didn't go back to get his hat from the lion's den!' So I said to her 'What do you want from this, is it the clothes, do you want to see him again, to provoke him again'. She had to see what she was doing because getting a woman off a violent relationship can be hard work. A violent relationship is the most intense relationship anybody can have. The whole excitement level of life is high and people really find it difficult to change that way of living. It's like coming off heroin.

So we have plenty of problems with the people in the house

and there are always questions of where the money's coming from, the lack of space, hassles with the authorities or with the government. But I can see that our ramshackle shelters do help. One of our mothers, Pat, wrote this poem called Damage and one way or another she speaks for all of us

People do not realise what others have been
    through,
The damage that's already done to us you really
    can't undo.
It leaves a scar within us, impossible to see,
It's rooted deep inside the heart, the pain won't
    let you free,
People say forget the past and leave it all behind,
As you'll get over it all right, left with a
    troubled mind.
I feel I have to relive my life and start all
    over again,
And finish where I started off when I was 9 or 10.
There is nothing in this world that I really
    want to see,
only to see
my children grown up and married happily.
When I have done all that I'll be getting on in
    years,
Then I can put my feet up and smile through all
    my tears.

So the deepest reason for the work that I'm doing lies in the damage I suffered. The most tragic thing that happened to me as a child was being unable to defend my own mother, I was too frightened. It may be irrational but it's impossible to forgive yourself for something like that and now it doesn't matter what problems are or what reasons people give me for closing the door of the refuge. The open door is for my mother. I remember how it felt and that is why the door will never close.

RABBI LIONEL BLUE
CONVERSATION WITH A CANDLE

Religious experience is not easy to talk about. Like taking a bath or being in love, it is a very private matter. I don't know what it means if you are outside it.

Sometime ago I was going home late on the underground. There were two people opposite and they were in love. 'I love you', he said. 'And I love you,' she answered, and so it went on all the way down the central line. All the rest of us in the carriage sniffed it was so boring. For us but not for them. For them it was obvious – each hackneyed phrase, each repetition brought new meaning and new insight. They were inside the experience and we were outside it – that was all. Everybody in love sees things that no one else can see, and they see, I think, more truly.

Loving God is not really different. You are either inside the experience or you aren't, and I don't really know how you get from one side to the other. I am a religious bureaucrat and I work surrounded by telephones, papers and files. I also help out at a synagogue. I am part of God's civil service I suppose, though after a day in the office I'm not all that civil. Like all ministers I go through very dry periods when God and I don't exactly quarrel but drift apart, and become more like those exhausted marriages when both sides have just stopped trying to speak to each other. I look at ordination photographs of student friends and I know it was not always like that. Sometime, somewhere, something gave one a shove but it can be very faint now. As a layman you don't have to bother so much with the rules and regulations, but if you are professionally religious the show has to go on whether you're in the mood or not. God works through you, even if he doesn't seem to work with you. You can't tell everybody to go home because the Almighty hasn't cancelled his plans just to keep an appointment with you.

Sometimes one tries to force a religious experience and give God a jog so to speak. I once stood before the ark desperately trying to think holy thoughts and all I could think of was something silly like: 'Ark, ark, the lark'. I was getting resigned to it going on like that for ever, and having to cover an awful lot of religious mileage on very little and low grade religious fuel, but then I had a bonus. I have got some hesitations about talking about this. It is not easy to hold on to an experience. People tell you it's subjective or it's an illusion, so that you begin to doubt yourself, and you start wondering. You have to be pretty stubborn these days to hold on and not deny what you've actually felt and seen. There is also the opposite danger. As the stock market goes down, interest in mysticism goes up, and at cocktail parties if I'm asked about my religious experiences, there's an awful temptation to inflate them and tart them up and put them in technicolour, and talk about them like someone going on and on about his operations. It's difficult being exact, just keeping to what one knows to be true.

My moment of truth happened to me at a shabby retreat centre in the Midlands. I'd agreed to give a lecture on Jewish prayer – not an easy thing to do. You can explain your religion so much that there's nothing left for yourself, you have explained it all away and talked it all out. You go to meetings and as a minister you naturally sit at the right hand of the chairman as is only proper. He says how nice it is you are a Jew and you say how nice it is he is a Christian or a Hindu or an Atheist. You have a cup of tea and it is all very nice, but where does it get you! I've been trying to work out why this lecture turned out so differently.

It was at a place called Spode, a conference centre run by some Dominicans, and it wasn't tarted up like a motel or an airport. Once upon a time it had been a pretty pretentious place but their money ran out so it never got completed. In any case it was built over a coal mine. When I got there they told me it was sinking steadily but safely, and you could see the cracks. I was really impressed because no one shooed me out of the kitchen, they gave me the keys of the bar, and one of the monks had eggstains on his robe.

This converted priory resting on a coal mine and surrounded by cooling towers reminded me of my own religious roots. I grew up in a Jewish Stepney before the war with its shabbiness and warmth. It was here that John Allen painted and when I paint I go back there too, because there are the holy places in my life, the deepest and most genuine things I know. In paint I can't falsify because I just don't know how.

I think what made my experience happen at Spode was the honesty of the people I met. They were girls and boys who were entering religious orders. Later on in their life they would learn how to evade, but at this point they were really open. I couldn't cheat them either – they were innocent, it would be like hurting a puppy or hitting a child, you just can't do it. Most of them hadn't quite got into their orders, and their uniforms showed it. There was something very touching about collapsed wimples, and robes which didn't cover their jeans. They reminded me of the old rabbis I used to know who tried so hard to be English and ended up looking more like Wyatt Erp than Saville Row. Anyway I tore up my notes and talked to them not about Judaism but about me, a Jew, and my difficulties in putting all the fragments of me together, my doubts as well as my beliefs. It was this dose of truth I think that brought on my own vision.

Late at night I was wandering down the corridors and I found myself in a room. There was a girl, a novice I think, sitting in the shadows, and a candle still burning after some experimental service or other. I asked myself what was it all about, our religious pretensions, and dressing up in bits of religious fancy dress, the unending processions which landed you back just where you started. Who was one trying to impress? At that point the candle said: 'me'. At least as I looked at it the word 'me' formed quite clearly in my mind. A bit doubtfully I thought I'd carry on and see where it took me. 'Is there anybody really there?' I asked. Though it's the only real religious question I felt a ninny because it was just like Margaret Rutherford in *Blithe Spirit* – one rap for 'yes' two raps for 'no'. The questions bubbled up in my mind, and in the light of the candle, the answers came too. It didn't just give light to the room, it enlightened me inside.

What was really going on in my life? Why had I met this person? Why had I suffered that disappointment? Both of us were remarkably chatty, not surprising I suppose because both of us were Jews. It went on for an hour, possibly two. But gradually the questions died down, and I was not learning any more. The candlelight seemed to be inside me too. I was actually enjoying the experience.

But I can't help being flippant because I don't know how else to take it. Like the boy and the girl on the underground the candle and I fell in love, rhyming moon and June with each other, or whatever the theological equivalents are. It doesn't matter how you explain it, provided you don't explain it away because it's uncomfortable. Religious institutions may look awfully solid, but they're only based on experiences like my candle – what Jacob dreamed up, or what Moses thought he saw in a burning bush. Very shaky and so firm at the same time that you stake your whole life on them.

This was how I thought about it on the way home. I had always known there was a place – a Garden of Eden if you like – but between it and me there were many doors, and I didn't know how to unlock them and I wasn't strong enough to break them. In that hour I knew that it was me who had created the doors and the locks and I could be in the garden whenever I accepted it. I didn't have to pass any examinations. I just had to take it – there it was and always had been. I also realised that I would never be alone again. This was a worrying thought, in some ways I liked it because I dislike being alone, but it was also worrying because it's not easy sharing one's life with anyone human or divine. This is a simple fact known to everyone who has ever tried to share a kitchen or flat or been married or lived in a community. And it was going to be difficult to make room to adjust to someone else in the centre of my being – in my heart.

I was curious as to whether the conversation would be localised in Spode. And I found out very quickly. I stopped at a motorway café on the way back. I bought a sandwich, and the bread immediately reminded me of the Jewish Matzah and Challah which I had shown the novices, and the communion wafers I had seen the novices eat. The candle came into my mind again and surrounded by cups and saucers the Almighty and I were in love again. I know how dreadful it sounds but there it is.

As a Rabbi I can't help feeling it's a pity this experience took place in a priory, and I can only thank God for reasons of professional etiquette that it didn't take place in a real church. I can't resume the conversation anywhere. It has a will of its own, and I've pursued it through orthodox synagogues with Hindus, Christians and especially Carmelites. It has also surfaced in a pub and on a train.

Lately it has centred on a room of prayer in the building where I work which is not often used. I feel considerably relieved that It's got integrated back into my normal life. I don't think I can say any more about it. It's either claptrap for you or you know what I'm talking about. I think lots of people have experiences like this. They are pretty normal. But most people don't use them, they throw them away, and waste them, because in a materialist society they get bullied by capitalists and revolutionaries alike. But with so many ideologies and religions going round, what can you believe in except your own experience. It's certainly created some problems. I always thought a religious experience would make me a nicer person. When I got back to London I was very nice for half an hour, and then I had a ferocious quarrel with everyone in sight. I think lots of people get disconcerted in this way. Another thing surprised me. I always thought an experience would make one graver, make me think more about sacrifice and sin. Well it didn't. I felt much younger, and much more kindly disposed to myself and others.

I had associated religion with pain; the happiness of it, the laughter in it, surprised me.

And what use has it been. Far more, in fact, than I expected. A book came out of it, my first. I am anxiety prone and the candlelight helps me to find a way through, to trust, more or less. Because of it some friends and I started a community without officers, committees, treasurers, or funds. We meet together on Friday evenings, bringing food, wine and candles, it has gone on now for two years.

The candle still enlightens me when I need it – at committee meetings for example when the real game is hidden under my own ego and illusion. I thought it would lead me away from the phone, the files and papers, but it doesn't. It gives them new life. I also give up my seat a little less grudgingly on buses. Gradually it has begun to show what success and failure really are – for me that is.

Perhaps its greatest help has been in funerals. I can talk more easily now when I take the service, because part of me has already gone ahead with the body, it started crossing that frontier in the room at Spode.

COLIN COWDREY
A HEALING TOUCH

For twenty-five years my life has been a narrow corridor surrounded by cricket. From the age of ten I became a 'cricketer to be watched' and I was never let out of the public sight. By thirteen, I had joined a team of boys four or five years my senior and had the thrill of making seventy-five in my first ever appearance at Lords. I was in the Kent side at seventeen, still a schoolboy and the youngest player to get a Kent cap. When I went up to Oxford, I became captain of the Oxford side. Then, totally unexpectedly, I was given a place as the baby of the MCC side chosen to go to Australia. I never dreamed of actually being chosen to play in a test match, but I thought that just the experience of even being twelfth man would be tremendous. But yet again I was thrown right in at the deep end. I hit really top form early and I was chosen to play in the first test match. Aged twenty-one and I had achieved my ambition of playing for England. Happily my career went from strength to strength. I was never really out of the side for the next twenty years. I became captain of Kent and captain of England.

I had reached the top of the tree and I had the determination to stay there until I retired, in 1975. But sometimes I reflect on those twenty-five years almost as if it were not me at all. I felt like two different people. One is the person I always was – a shy, simple man with a single-minded ideal of trying to be just the best cricketer in the world. The other was being a public figure which I couldn't control because you are constantly being swayed about by other people and particularly the media. You can say something quite innocently about Australian umpires, maybe at a little dinner in Margate, and next morning you are news and controversy in Melbourne.

Very early on in my career, I found out how exposed life at the top can be and so lonely. On your way there, everyone is supporting you. Even your rivals are patting you on the back and wishing you luck. But as soon as you arrive there, a million hands suddenly disappear. I found everyone wanted to win themselves and they wanted me out. All the time I knew I was being studied and watched. I could walk into a test match and know exactly what field there would be for each separate bowler. And they would know that I would know. It is like a tremendous game of chess. When I was playing well I could always find a surprise move to nonplus the attack. But when I played badly, it could be a vicious spiral down. The pressures came over the top of you and threatened to submerge you.

I was so anxious to do well that I became terribly afraid at times of some matches and had confrontations with bowlers who I thought had the whip-hand. I built up a fear of falling short or failing completely. I had to fight a deep down desire to pull out, the temptation to find some injury perhaps that would provide me with an apparently honourable excuse and reason for being unavailable. I think some people make the mistake of thinking that sport is in some way static, that once you get to the top, you stay at the top. The truth is that it is so easy to hit a bad patch and never recover, and that a really serious injury is always just round the corner. And it was exactly this combination – loss of form, a bad patch and an irritating number of minor injuries, that led me by chance into the world of Christian healing.

In 1970, after fifteen years as captain of Kent, I had the huge thrill of leading them to victory in the county championship. Afterwards I relinquished the captaincy of Kent. My aim was to enjoy a few more leisurely years in county cricket, and perhaps to join the élite sixteen who had made the coveted hundred hundreds. But I ran into one of these bad patches. I lost form. In the space of a few weeks I broke a bone in my finger diving for a catch; I half pulled a hamstring; I was hit rather nastily on the knee and again on the ankle; a couple of bouncers on a wet wicket went into my ribs and a cold wind had got into my back. None of these knocks stopped me playing but it was irksome. It took ages to get out of bed every morning. It was probably the worst period of my life.

Although I had no first-hand knowledge, the idea of healing was not totally new to me. As a child, I remember being particularly arrested by the gospel stories – the idea of Christ healing a man of his blindness by a single touch of his hands on eyes that had never seen before and curing the lame and the sick simply by acknowledging their faith and touching them. My own religious upbringing was fairly traditional and orthodox. I came from a Christian home where churchgoing was the naturally accepted thing, and I think I have always had an active Christian faith. Even when I was coming to the end of my time at Oxford it was not beyond the bounds of possibility that I might have been ordained.

I had a friend at Oxford who had a great influence on me, though at the time I could not take his ideas very seriously at all. He wanted to be a doctor and he had a great mission for what he called Christian healing. He died tragically in his early thirties. He was always badgering me about healing and to my shame, I really didn't allow myself to really look into his ideas. I even probably quietly thought of him as a bit of a crank. But he had planted the seeds of an idea somewhere in the back of my mind, because nearly twenty years later I found myself at the home of Mary Rogers, and really not at all sure what I had let myself in for.

I had heard about Mary Rogers from several people, and I suppose that the effect was rather like hearing a new word. You gradually hear more and more people saying it and it's only a matter of time before you're using it yourself. I think my personal barrier to healing finally broke down after a conversation I had with a Kent supporter, who was an eminent businessman. He explained how he had been under terrible pressure at his work and how this healer, Mary Rogers, had guided him through a really bad period. His was not a dramatic cure. I knew he had his feet firmly planted on the ground, and that if she could have so much relevance to his life, she couldn't be all that much of a crank. But I was still sceptical right up to the moment I met her, then all my fears were banished. I couldn't get over the fact that she was so ordinary and behaved so normally. She seemed just like any other mother, happy and contented with her children and her grandchildren and her country garden in Sussex. She is a Lancastrian with a warm sense of fun and she soon made me feel very relaxed.

After a while she suggested that we move to what she called her little sanctuary. The walls were surrounded by flowers, statues and pictures and various religious objects. One corner was entirely covered by cards and postcards. Afterwards I learnt that these were all from patients throughout the world, some of whom she had never met. Mary seemed able to help people just by touching and holding the affected parts on the photographs.

Fortunately she had no idea who I was. It was a great relief to feel that I was not going to have a special show laid on because I was well known. I sat in the little sanctuary and as she put her hands on my head my eyes were riveted to a striking painting of Our Lord. I was now a little more relaxed but still sceptical. After a few moments of quiet calm, her healing hand, the right one, was placed flat on my back, exactly over the area that was causing me trouble. I was conscious of an increasing warmth. After a little while, she questioned me about my right hand and put her right hand around the damaged finger. Again I was conscious of warmth. She went on to each one of my injuries in turn, without any word from me. She found the calves of my legs were tight and asked me if I did outdoor work. With a poker face I conceded that I lived an active life out of doors.

I could not get over the fierce heat in her hand, so much so that I went to touch it and was astonished to find that there was no extraordinary warmth at all, if anything it was a little cooler than my own. The healing heat was something from within. Staring at the picture on the wall, I couldn't help thinking back to my pictures of Christ healing the sick or curing the blind man just by touching his eyes. I felt I could understand something of the feeling of the woman in the Gospel story who was cured of a haemorrhage. She could only just manage to touch the hem of Jesus's garment in the jostling crowd surrounding him. He could not possibly have felt the touch of her hand, but he stopped, knowing that the power had gone out of him.

I was so moved by the precision of her diagnosis and the heat of healing in her hands that I confessed who I was. She was interested, but was not a cricket fan. Afterwards I sat in the chair for about half an hour. There was no flash of light like it happened to St Paul on the Damascus road. I was conscious of a great feeling of peace and well-being. I felt no noticeable difference in my aches and pains, yet within a day or two, I found myself unaccountably fitter and freer, so much so that I cancelled my regular treatments and I have never really been committed to them since.

No one really knew about my healing. I didn't talk about it or feel the need to preach about it. It was a very personal thing and it left me feeling pretty staggered. My link with Mary Rogers has remained firm ever since. And in my cricket I still had peaks to climb especially achieving the coveted hundred hundreds. And in 1974, I was recalled to the England side in Australia, just a few months before I retired. By coincidence Mary was visiting Melbourne, and I was able to see her working at close quarters. There were some quite remarkable dramatic cases of healing and everyone who came in touch with her went away moved and uplifted.

It has to be said of course that some would go away apparently untouched, but whilst I cannot prove it I am convinced that they would all have been helped in some way. Mary would say, with very real humility, that we must remember that God heals in his own good time and that she was just the hands through which the power of the spirit can be shown. It is not for you or for me to judge or to say who is going to benefit or when. I regard it as my immense good fortune to have seen the power of healing and to have received it myself. I am still trying to piece things together. I cannot explain it but I can say in the words of the blind man whose sight was restored by Jesus 'I know not of these things, but one thing I know; whereas I was blind, now I see'.

PAUL YATES

FRAGMENTS

Long ago in Belfast when I was five or six I used to play the game of the splendid death. There were four of us usually. We gathered on a hill by the streets where we lived. The game began with one of us being chosen as the gunner. The gunner would then move to the bottom of the hill and take up his position – kneeling or lying on his belly, a pretend rifle trained in his arms. One by one we charged down towards him to die our splendid deaths. Some charged with pistols or sword, some with grenades or bayonet fixed. Carefully we anticipated which part of us the gunner was aiming at and clutching it appropriately, wheeled and fell on the pretend bullets. Thus we died, over and over again. Glorious, splendid, pretend deaths. Safe in the knowledge we could always get up again, and he who in the gunner's opinion had died the most splendid death changed places with the gunner for the following round – and so the game continued.

As children we had no knowledge of the realities of violent death – our only frame of reference lay in cinema westerns, adventure stories, comic strips and television. So we played games. But that was a long time ago in Northern Ireland. There is nothing very splendid about violent death there now. Nothing very splendid about being blown to pieces in a restaurant or a bar. Not much glory in being shot in the back when it is dark, or caught in a crossfire. It's no longer a game we are playing. The gunner is not prepared to change places with anyone. He is using live ammunition and doesn't intend that any of us should get up again.

The casual observer spies with his little eye
Something beginning with B
   barricades; sleeping across the mouth of a nation gagged
   and bound with barbed-wire.
Something beginning with A
   assassins; emptying their rifles into the darkness, aiming
   at everything.
Something beginning with E
   explosions; their ghosts at each other's throats, breaking
   the chairs and the tables and all the rest of us.
Something beginning with P
   pieces of people; doing what pieces of people do, just
   lying there.
Something beginning with M
   mess; like broken glass in your eyes stopping you from
   doing anything about it.

That poem was one of a series I have written on the conflict
in Ulster. I started writing poetry at the age of nine and have
always experienced the sense of being two people. One, the
poet; and the other, me. So when I talk about my poetry I feel
as if I am speaking on behalf of someone else. The only time I
feel alive is when I am lost before my typewriter, furiously trying
to keep up with what's happening inside me, possessed with
images and trying to write them down before they escape.

As the poet I feel isolated from other people. Indeed in my
school days I was not easily accepted and there is still a general
myth that anyone who is a poet – and I mean a poet and not
merely someone who writes poetry – is in some way weird or
insane. Poets are different because for them the world of the
imagination is more real than the world around them in daily
life. I was even more isolated because my ideas differed so vastly
from the traditionalist approach I found all around me in Ulster.
Isolated though I was, I still shared with my friends the common
preoccupations of adolescence – alcohol, sex and music.

We were all part of the last generation to experience 'peace' in Northern Ireland. We were sixteen years old and still at school. We danced, we drank cheap wine, smoked French cigarettes, rolled around all night just coming home. We thought nothing of walking home across Belfast's city centre – taking short cuts through back streets and alleyways – or hitching to and from the coast. We had the open road, the music and the moon. There was no threat of danger, no gunman lurking in the dark, no bomb ticking away beneath the tables where we were eating and drinking.

That kind of spirit and casual freedom of movement no longer exists in Northern Ireland. Those generations which followed mine have inherited a society where death and violence are an everyday occurrence. City centres are like ghost towns with horizons that halt where the violence begins.

I remember coming out of a bar deep in the heart of Belfast. Leaning on the corner to smoke a cigarette I looked up and down the street. Row after row of shop windows and doorways bricked up, boarded up, filled in. Everything was sunk in a pale grey light, not a soul in sight. A discarded newspaper blew across the road, clouds of dust followed from nearby demolition sites. A stray dog trotted nervously along the pavement. In the distance I could hear the sound of gunfire and ambulance sirens.

The dog stopped beside me, it's ears leaned back in the direction of the guns and sirens. It began a low almost imperceptible howl which gradually got louder. The howl came in unison with the ambulance sirens. The dog's body trembled, its head moved from side to side unable to understand what had triggered the howling mechanism in its brain. Its eyes were filled with fear and confusion. It looked up at me but saw no answers. The buses were off, the trains were off. Not a soul in sight. Just me and this dog howling at my feet. The whole scene took on a sense of inertia like it was a dream or a nightmare. Everything dirty, everything ruined. Each of us trapped under a sky made of stone. Confused. Unable to move. Unable to understand. Howling.

That there is to be a new definition of the term
'death by natural causes' which shall now include
the following points
Death by explosion
Death by gun shot
Death by blunt instrument or mob
Death by suffocation in hood

Death by terror or by fear or
by pain or by hideous torture
or
by being the wrong colour
the wrong creed
the wrong sort and in
the wrong time
at
the wrong place.

The wrong place – that is exactly what Ulster seemed to me at that time. There I was, the poet continually writing and the other me ignoring the violence around me. After all Cézanne had painted his apples during the Franco-Prussian war and people remember Cézanne's apples but how many recall the Franco-Prussian war? However the conflict in Ulster was gradually catching up with me. I remember sitting in the middle of the night punching out lines like 'kiss like a strawberry bitten in half on the tongue'. In the distance I could hear the sound of gunfire and explosions. It isn't easy to write 'kiss like a strawberry bitten in half on the tongue' when all around you everything is going bang. The conflict, the mess came to lie heavy on my tongue and in my stomach. It was like wanting to be sick and not being able to. I carried it around inside me.

You
can kill me for gold anytime;
Drown or
strangle me for a woman;

Set fire to

me because I
lost all your money at the races;
But

You
trying to kill me for peace
is
just enough to make me keep struggling all
through the peace between

wars

Until the next one, and
then you've had it.

So the conflict grew. Atrocity heaped upon atrocity. Bombing.
Murder. Torture. Sectarian assassination. The violence took aim
on everything. The mess hung upon our back like a suit of wet
clothes. The statements of politicians were as useless as the
warnings printed on the sides of cigarette packets: 'Warning
by Her Majesty's Government – Terrorism can damage your
health. Give it up you know it makes sense.'

The constant press and television coverage of the conflict
came to have an anaesthetic effect. We became immune to further
horrors. A terrible apathy grew. We'd suffered so much, little
more could hurt us. We didn't even take in the news. People in
bars continued drinking and talking during the reports. We
no longer bothered to look up. We had heard it all before. Heads
remained lowered between glasses and conversation. We had
adapted to having violence as a natural background or sometimes foreground to our daily lives. Another man dead meant
simply that – another man dead.

But it is not all war in Ulster, no matter what the papers say.
The wheel of fortune still rolls round corners without looking.
Lovers make love, day breaks and night falls without hurting
anyone. People still contend with all the other ordinary and
extraordinary complexities of life. But this struggle with the
ordinary and the extraordinary in spite of the conflict – this

spirit of getting on with life no matter what, this is the true heroism of the Ulster people. These people have suffered incredible damage to their spirit and society yet they refuse to give in. Their heroism ranges from the continual high efficiency of hospitals, doctors, surgeons and nurses to the resoluteness of Belfast city centre workers who despite the harshest bombing campaigns turn up for work as usual.

The first poem I actually wrote about the Ulster conflict was *Bloody Friday*. I was in Belfast that day when the bombs began to go off – first one, then two, then three, again and again until I lost count. We were hemmed in, jostled in all directions only to find the way blocked, driven backwards and forwards across the city centre. Eventually seeking some avenue of escape I found myself at Oxford Street. The bus station was burning. Wrecked in an explosion. Between the flames and the debris I saw something odd. A piece of human flesh, it seemed pinned in the wreckage. The sight of this was what finally moved me to begin writing the war poems.

> After
> seeing it; that
> thing I didn't recognise as a piece of man.
> I
> moved to stand behind the crowd.
> That
> thing
> was something stolen from a man.
> Something that could not be replaced. I
> tried to
> imagine the thief. I
> tried to imagine him smoking or eating or
> drinking or doing something you need
> a head and a face for.
> And there are no poems which put men
> back together again.
> We didn't have a chance.

The killing goes on, the terror goes on. But they can't kill all of us and gradually more and more people are reacting against it – determined that violence and terror will not win – that no political cause or patriotism shall be the façade for the murder of innocent people.

When I finished writing the war poems I experienced a sense of relief – I felt somehow I could not be touched again as deeply as before by the conflict. But that's not true after all. I am still shocked and incensed at the futility of the violence. Some people have told me that my poetry expressed their anger and frustration. If that is true – if, in some way, the poems have enabled other people to release their frustration and grief, then I feel it has achieved something.

CICELY SAUNDERS
A WINDOW IN YOUR HOME

'I'll be a window in your home' was the promise given to me in 1948 by David Tasma, a Pole from the Warsaw Ghetto, and one of the patients who are the real founders of the hospice where I work. His £500 for this window was the first gift, and gave us a symbol of openness, of looking in and of looking out. The hospice offers special skills to those for whom the busy, acute ward is really no longer the best place for them to be. Indeed, at any time half of our patients are in their own homes. The whole building speaks of welcome and of space for people to be themselves. Most people are afraid of pain, dependence or death, and yet these can so often be overcome or may lead to some of the most valuable moments of life. Often it is the patients who teach and build us, not the other way round. However ill or disabled they may be, no one need be only on the receiving end. Those who care for them must recognise and relieve their symptoms and honour their independence.

Nineteen years after that promise of the window the hospice was finally built round it. Just as it was David who gave us the symbol of openness, so others added the insights that came from seeing their different needs and achievements. I was a social worker but I had nursing experience and to learn more I worked in the evenings in a small hospital for terminal care. I began to see what could be done to help people like David and this finally impelled me into becoming a doctor. It was a long apprenticeship but all along the way I was meeting people, patients who were my friends.

There was Mrs G. She spent the last seven years of her life in hospital, losing her sight and finally nearly all independent movement. But towards the end she was so alert and interested in everyone that she was the best centre of gossip in the hospital. Then there was Louie who had fragile bones and had spent her whole life in bed. Louie was eager to discuss every detail and hope with me, to check over plans from the patient's point of view, and to promise 'I'll be round about your hospice always because I know what it's like to need it.' Though they did not live to see our hospice opened, their ideas, their spirit and, I believe, their prayers, are built into the bricks.

Among the many patients there was one who was different – one friendship which during the last few weeks took on a new dimension. Antoni was Polish like David, and we met when he was already mortally ill. The first six months or so were occupied with his fight to live – at least until his daughter had passed her examinations. His wife had died four years before and though he had friends he had no other near relatives. He spent long hours of silence in the ward. I think he was naturally a rather silent person but he told me once that English *was* his eighth best language. I found later, too, how much of that time was spent in prayer.

At last his daughter heard about her examinations and I went to congratulate her while she was visiting him. His eyes filled with tears and I took his hand. He kissed it and she said, 'My father has so much love for you doctor,' and he said, 'I do not know how to express it and please do not be offended'. I said, 'Indeed no, I am grateful,' and left them.

Later that day he asked me, very definitely, if he was going to die. It would have been an insult not to be honest to a person of his faith and his courage and I told him 'yes'. He waited a moment and then he said, 'Was it hard for you to tell me that?' I said 'Well – yes – it was,' and he said, 'Thank you – it is hard to be told but it is hard to tell too, thank you.' We went on talking and suddenly we were meeting in a new way. He said, 'It is years and years since I just sat and talked to somebody. I have forgotten how to.' After that, because I knew how much I would forget, I kept a diary of our talks. For a long time I had been writing out a prayer each day based on a morning reading. To these daily prayers I now added the diary of what Antoni said to me, of how things were. I spent what time I could with him, but we were never alone, we were always surrounded by other people in the ward. I could never stay longer than an hour at most but he said, 'I want you beside me all day long; but for me, this is enough.' So time – just over three weeks in all – was too short to waste, and it wasn't wasted. I don't think we failed to say anything we wanted to say; nor was there anything I regretted and wanted unsaid. Looking back it's the positive and peaceful side that remains with me now, and I am surprised to read how hard it was sometimes.

Early in those three weeks I remember him saying to me, 'When I was a child and I saw a toy in a shop I said "I want that, I want it *now*," and all my life I am like that – but now I see what I want, and I know it is not for me'. And later, 'I can give you nothing, nothing but sorrow'. But gradually I know he realised how much *was* given to me in that short, cramped time, I remember writing in my diary how I tried to tell him what it meant to me. That morning I wrote a prayer from the text:

'First of August. "Faith worketh by love."
O Lord, I pray that our love may be of
faith and may help to faith. O Lord,
please may it help him to know Thee
better and to go forth in peace to Thee.'

Then that night I wrote: 'Except there are problems. I said that to know he cared was a rest to my heart and always would be. He said he was sure he was better and perhaps he would have longer. I said we couldn't ever be alone and I couldn't come as often as I wanted. He said "I am waiting till you come".'

Our meeting was filled so full and so deeply in that short time that it not only gave me a gift of love such as I had not known, but also a new sense of time and of timing. I know how far a relationship can travel in a few weeks, what peace and wisdom can be achieved and handed on at the end of a hard and seemingly frustrated life. I know how independent we can be of circumstances, even in a time of great physical weakness. We both wanted him to go on living but the moment came when I stopped praying for him to stay a little longer. I wrote: 'O Lord he is weary and I couldn't ask him to stay for me. Please take him home in Thy perfect time – and I don't ask for any more; but take my hands off.' Soon after that I found that everything had gone quiet and our last few days were filled with a strange peace. Just before he too found peace, while he still felt he could only hurt me, I remember saying, 'Don't look so sad'. He answered, still with his somewhat wry humour, 'How should I look, amused? But I have peace, I am grateful to you and to God for that'. And the day before he died, finally, when I said, 'Please believe me, it isn't only I who has given to you, but you who have given to me, and I am grateful', he answered, 'I believe you'.

That was almost the last thing he said to me. But the next afternoon, an hour before he died, when I had to leave to go on with the day's work, he suddenly smiled at me, for the last time. I wrote in my diary that night: 'I am not certain of all that was in it – not sorrow at all – he looked so happy – and there was certainly a gleam of amusement – strong somehow.' In fact as I realised, rather indignantly at first, he looked amused. He was seeing answers, seeing Him he had believed in without sight, seeing that he need not worry about me – I would be comforted. I was, but it took a long time before in the end it all came together, and I found peace again. We had no past, no ordinary things to remember but somehow the strength of being together at the end of his hard life, of being kept in a kind of solitude in the midst of a busy ward and the joy of finding each other in the very time of parting, belong to all I aim to do now.

This is a story of love and parting, a kind of song, and the years since have been full of his music. But I was not lifted easily at the beginning. All through that bleak first year I remember stopping at the ward door and thinking, 'Lord, I can't go in, it hurts too much', and then looking up to the crucifix and letting it hold me. But yet it was through the demands of the work and all I found that we could do to help patients that I finally integrated this experience into my life. It was, however, often difficult to keep going – even with Mrs G and Louie and other patients and friends to support me.

The Courtauld Gallery was one of my refreshing places. Antoni had told me that he sang tenor but had spoiled his voice by smoking and that he loved Schubert and Strauss. I began to find pictures that went with his music. There was a portrait of a sixteenth-century man, so extraordinarily like Antoni, that drew me back over and over again and which matched the yearning of Strauss's *Morgen*. Also one of Monet's pictures came together with a swinging song of Schubert's and sent me home lifted up once more.

I think the most important thing I learned was that in no work with people is all the giving on one side. And the hospice is built on a recognition of how much our patients and families have to give us, as well as to each other. This is not a 'good work' setting out to help some 'poor people'. Pity is dangerously near to despising and denigration.

So the hospice was founded and grows still – from the relationships that can develop in mortal illness or long disability or age. Jesus was right when he said, 'Blessed are those that mourn for they shall be comforted – made strong'.

No one seems able to understand that the hospice is so living as well as so peaceful until they come and see it. Of course we are not perfect, but just as Antoni and I lived our life together, believing that it was held in hands stronger than ours, and because I could make sure that he had no pain and had the freedom to be himself, so we are giving peace and space to those who come to the hospice and they do most truly use it.

Grief can be great and to hear the forlorn crying of the parted does not cease to hurt. But I have shared this grief and know that there is something much stronger behind it all – not an answer, no explanation, but a presence. We believe, many of us here, that this is the presence of a God who has shared our suffering with no more than the equipment of a man and who, having come through, shares the sorrows of all men and will transform them. In the end we will know the answers and we will also find, like Antoni, we can be amused.

NEVILLE JAYAWEERA

AN AWESOME ENCOUNTER

Six years ago, something happened to me which had the effect of completely transforming and reversing the values I had lived by till then. I come from Sri Lanka, formerly known as Ceylon. I was born to a strongly traditional and somewhat dogmatic Buddhist family. I was educated in two leading Christian missionary colleges in Colombo where, among other things, I acquired a strong antipathy towards the Church in particular, and towards Christianity and Christians in general. I was a student of western philosophy in the university where, after graduating, I taught logic and metaphysics. But after a year, I abandoned the university for the better paid and more prestigious administrative corps which was then known as the Ceylon Civil Service.

In the Civil Service, at the age of 25, I launched out on what turned out to be a meteoric career. I threw myself into my work with an energy that was almost demonic. I worked 16 hours a day and drove my colleagues and subordinates with a ruthless-ness and intolerance that were frightening. Promotions came thick and fast. I became General Manager of the GALOYA Development Board. Then I was appointed Government Agent of the Northern District. Next I became Government Agent of the Eastern District. Then the Prime Minister requested my appointment as the Director General of the Ceylon Broadcasting Corporation.

I loved wielding power and basking in the pomp and glamour that went with it. But all this success had transformed me into an intolerably arrogant and supercilious little bounder and, with another twenty years to go before retirement, I had virtually reached the top of the administrative ladder. And then my world crashed and with it my career and my personal life.

In May 1970 a General Election was held in my country. During the election campaign the left dominated opposition had promised the trade unions that if they were returned to power, I would be sent out of office. You see, over the years, my uncompromising stand on discipline and work-output had reduced me to an object of intense hate to the trade unions. In their minds I was a reactionary, an incurable imperialist, a fascist. The opposition won the election overwhelmingly and within twenty-four hours of their victory my family and I had to go into hiding in order to escape the wrath of the trade unionists who were looking for me to mete out summary justice.

Before I went into hiding, I handed in my resignation from the Broadcasting Corporation to the new Prime Minister. She accepted my resignation but was very gracious about it all, and ordered that a Royal Commission be appointed to investigate the charges being levelled against me. She retained me in the Civil Service and gave me a small jungle district to administer far away from Columbo.

Because my child was very young I had to leave my family behind and was living away from my friends in this remote jungle environment. Life was an indescribable agony. I had to watch helplessly as one time friends and colleagues fell over each other in their drive to destroy me. Not a day passed when a newspaper did not carry some new accusation levelled against me by some politician or trade union leader. And there I was a silent spectator, embittered and helpless, with resentment boiling up inside me against this calculated campaign to denigrate me. The world I had built up for myself lay in shambles around me. My ego was being crushed into the ground every day and my pride lay shattered.

Night after night, for days and weeks on end I could not sleep. Copious draughts of alcohol and even tranquillisers gave me no relief. As a last resort, I took to experimenting with yoga meditation. But whenever I sat crossed-legged, closed my eyes and tried to quieten my thoughts my mind went into an even worse tumult. However, from the very first day I noticed something curious happening. Whenever I closed my eyes I began to notice a flame-like glow at a point between my eyes in the centre of my forehead, and a dark blur in the middle of the glow. After a few days I noticed that this dark blur had taken on a distinctly human form. It was the image of a man dressed in a long robe standing upright, facing me with his arms stretched out and apart, waiting as if to receive me, clearly silhouetted against the glow in the background. On about the seventh night of my experiment with yoga meditation, the thought suddenly flashed into my mind that the image in my mind's eye was an exact resemblance of a painting of Jesus Christ I had seen framed on a wall somewhere.

My immediate reaction was one of anger for the realisation that this was Jesus touched off my deep antipathy towards Christianity. And then, quite involuntarily and contrary to my conscious impulse, I blurted out 'My Lord, forgive me'. Then the dam burst. I went into convulsions of uncontrollable sobbing. At some point I had changed my position from sitting cross-legged to kneeling, with my head bowed low as if in a position of obeisance. And then I passed out. I awoke, to find myself curled up like a foetus on the ground, and bathed in perspiration. I looked at the time. It was 1.30 in the morning. So I climbed into bed and drifted again into a deep sleep.

I awoke at 6.30 am and literally sprang out of bed. I felt a tingling sensation through my body. I felt light as a feather, as if I were levitating. I felt clean inside as if a reservoir of foetid puss that had been locked up inside me for years had all been drained out. Then I realised that I had no load on my chest. I seemed to have lost the capacity to hate. Resentments that I had been nursing inside me for months seemed to have evaporated. I walked to the large bay window of my room and looked out. The morning sun filtering in through the trees seemed like liquid music. I seemed to discover a new world existing outside the miserable little dungeon of my ego in which I had been held captive for forty years. For the first time in my life I had come to know the meaning of that simple three-letter word 'joy'. 'Yes, this indeed was joy'.

I did not connect any of these things with Jesus Christ or with religion or with my meditation experience of the previous night. I was able to connect them only through a series of extraordinary coincidences that followed. The next day I received a letter from a friend of the family, an Anglican Bishop, saying that I had been in his thoughts a great deal lately, that he had in fact been praying for me and felt compelled to send me a little booklet. In fact the book was a poem, *The Hound of Heaven*, by Francis Thomson:

I fled him down the nights and down the days;
I fled him down the arches of the years;
I fled him down the labyrinthine ways of my
own mind, and in the midst of tears I hid from him.

'The Hound of Heaven' had indeed finally overpowered me. The following day I had another letter, this time from a Hindu friend, enclosing a book which he had picked up the previous day, *The Imitation of Christ*, by Thomas A. Kempis: 'My son, hear my words, words of great sweetness, surpassing all the learning of philosophers and wise men of this world. My words are spirit and life, and cannot be weighed by the understanding of man.' It was on reading this book that I realised that Christ had in fact come into my own life, and that the ecstasy, the joy and peace I now knew, and the release from captivity to my ego, were all His work.

Then, consciously and deliberately, I yielded to Christ. But the old intellectual in me still demanded proof and restrained me from total faith. It occurred to me that this could be just a nervous breakdown. Or perhaps it was a clever but sub-conscious device of my mind to find an escape from my prob-lems. So I decided to watch myself closely for some time. I noticed that the joy and the inner peace not only remained but deepened. I felt more integrated as a person than I had ever been before. My work output and efficiency increased greatly. My mind remained utterly rational. All problems of personal relations disappeared. I lost the capacity for anger and felt constantly a deep humility. I had to conclude then that my experience that night had not been a mere quirk of my mind, that Christ was in fact real and that He had come into my life for good.

I was now driven by an overpowering desire to share and proclaim Christ. This was no small undertaking in a predominantly Buddhist society. I started preaching in public. The Buddhists reacted initially with incredulity. They said I had gone mad. Then they responded with scorn and ridicule. But I persisted. Then the storm broke. My family and I soon became the object of a terrible campaign of persecution and harassment. My detractors engaged a private detective agency to uncover all that was sordid in my past personal life and came up with an eighteen-page document which purported to set out all that was ugly in my life. They sent this document as a Christmas present to my wife. They also circulated it to the Prime Minister, Cabinet Ministers, the Archbishop and all bishops and parish priests, and to the newspapers. Even clandestine press advertisements were mobilised to destroy me.

The focus of this cruel and pitiless campaign was my wife. The aim was to destroy my home and silence my evangelical activities. My wife's reaction was astonishing. I had drifted away from her over the years. In fact my marriage had been one of the first victims of my insatiable desire for success. But I had always respected my wife as the most wonderful woman I had met. Faced with this onslaught, she rose to incredible heights. We rediscovered our relationship as husband and wife, drew closer to each other, and for the first time since we married, converted what had been a house into a Christian home.

Meanwhile the Royal Commission had sat for one whole year and cleared my name. The Minister for Public Administration got up in parliament and paid me a lofty tribute for my conduct as a public servant. I was rehabilitated in the eyes of the new government and was being recalled to hold high office again, to resume the career that had been interrupted for two years. But the tinsel attractions of high office no longer interested me and I retired prematurely. A year later I accepted an invitation to work for the World Association of Christian Communication in England.

Now my wife, our daughter Manohari and I live in a quiet suburb in Kent. We are a happy and contented Christian home. No more the striving, the straining and the climbing after success. This does not mean, however, that I have retreated from involvement or abdicated my responsibilities to society. It only means that we have no ambitions of our own except to serve and be where Christ wants us at the moment.

What are my philosophical views now? Have I abrogated the tools of philosophical analysis? Most emphatically – no! But I now know that there is a whole realm of reality and truth to which neither science nor philosophical analysis can give me access. I say so because I have had a glimpse into this other reality. It is this other reality that gives meaning to my life, my relationships, my values. And what about the problems posed by some of the apparently absurd claims of the Bible? How do I deal with them? The answer is that I have no problems with the Bible, for when one has met at first hand the person of Christ, no absurdity, no contradiction however blatant, can prevail against or vitiate that awesome encounter.

BILL EDWARDS
A NAGGING DOUBT

My story is of a conflict. It has been an undercurrent that nagged away at me for many years. It is only now as I start my fifties that I feel I can look back and begin to define the nature of this conflict. It was, and to some extent still is, a tension between the wish for material success – money, power, position – and a recognition, largely unconscious, that those are not the true values for life. During my life these two opposing forces drove me to a point which some might characterise as breakdown.

My ambition for success started in a conventional enough way. I had some success at school – good examination results and so on – but the first real landmark was in 1950 when I left Oxford with a degree in law. It was a good degree and it started to open doors for me. Because of it, just after I was called to the bar in London and before I started my intended career as a barrister, I was offered a visiting lectureship at a university on the west coast of Canada in Vancouver. To travel across the great plains of Canada, to pass the lakes and on into the Rocky Mountains towards the Pacific, that was an irresistible adventure for me at the age of 26.

Instead of staying one year in Canada as originally planned I stayed two years. It was a full life. The academic atmosphere was enriching. I was teaching bright and interested people, some of them older than myself. I had lots of free time for ski-ing, sailing, swimming and fishing. I drove throughout North America, visited Mexico and worked as a cook in the Yukon. I enjoyed the hospitality of well-to-do lawyers and businessmen and their families. Soon I began to acquire a feeling of relish for the material comforts which their successful lives gave them and my ambitions drove me on to achieve a similar success for myself. The only dilemma I was conscious of was whether to return to a barrister's practice in Britain or to continue to live in North America, where, it was clear, the real money was to be made. I decided to go to Harvard and study American company law as that would open more doors. For me education was still essentially a means to earn a high salary. My decision paid off.

Harvard opened the door to Wall Street, to the world of big business, finance and glittering rewards. I became an official immigrant to the United States. I took a job in the Head Office of a well-known international company and settled into the busy, lucrative, sophisticated life of an up-and-coming young lawyer executive. The work was fascinating, demanding and infinitely varied. The life was full in terms of both work and play. New York was certainly for me a city of great energy and great excitement.

After two years, family reasons required my return to England. There was no real choice in it for me. If I were to fulfil my responsibilities to other persons, I had to return. It would be wrong to create the impression that I regarded the return as a sacrifice. I could chase success as well in Britain as in America, although at a somewhat lower material level. Still, in the context of a lower standard of living, that did not matter.

The circumstances made it easy for me. I simply transferred to the London office of the same company and settled in quickly as an equally up-and-coming young executive. I rose quickly to become a director of the British subsidiary company. The fringe benefits of a directorship in Britain can be an Aladdin's cave of goodies – especially if one can close one's eyes to the obscenity of ostentation which so often accompanies the appointment. And it's quite easy to close one's eyes in this way. I had been through an expensive education by now into a world where not only should one succeed, but also one should be seen to succeed. And the way that one proved it to oneself and one's friends was by the size of one's slice of cake. My slice was very big – but a nagging doubt began when I contemplated the years that lay ahead of me.

It would be thirty years before I would retire in the normal course of events. Thirty years of a comfortable well-paid existence. It is difficult to define what this feeling at the time was, but two aspects of it are quite clear. While I could see ahead this prospect of thirty years of status, high salaries and all that went with it, I was also aware of the effects of such a life on some of those who had enjoyed these benefits. I remember two senior men who were in constant struggle. I was aware that each was playing a role. With power and position it is easy to forget that one is just oneself – that one is not the role which one plays. But I found myself being drawn into a feeling of false identity. I began not to like the feeling.

Another aspect was the isolation from the ordinary human world. For example, in the mornings I would walk across St James's Park to my club and swim in a colonnaded pool and then be picked up by a chauffeur-driven car to take me to the office. I felt isolated by my role and I felt guilty at my privilege. I had never experienced the ordinary hurts and worries of most people and strange as it may seem that itself became a source of pain. What actually happened was that I reached a breaking point – I didn't know what I really wanted to do but I knew I had to get out of that position – so I resigned.

I must not give the impression that my resignation in some way proved that I had resolved a problem for it was the beginning of the most intense years of doubt. I felt unable to tell the chairman of the company what I was really feeling, so I said that I wanted to take up a career at the bar. It was the kind of thing that would be more understandable to a career-orientated man. I was still in too much awe of the role of a company chairman to try to tell him that I didn't know what I wanted. I needed to get away to find out who I was without all the padding of high executive life. The evening of my resignation I was given a typical company send-off. Everyone shook my hand, then a little later I was alone with my thoughts and I wept, not for nostalgia nor for relief, but because I'd actually taken a step and now my underlying feelings were breaking through.

So I left and went to the bar, still in doubt, still unresolved. I knew this wasn't what I wanted to do and saw it as a stepping stone to something else but I didn't really know what this something else was going to be. All I knew was that it was not going to be the pursuit of material ambition. I didn't settle at the bar but took up a job I was offered in education for management. The odd thing was, I knew it would fail and that I had to fail with it. I had begun to have a sense that I had to suffer. It sounds morbid, but it was a recognition that I had to try to meet life without any of the layers that had overlarded me during the years. Suffering can tear away those layers and make it possible to meet oneself. My suffering was the questioning of my own worth. I had turned away from success and now was experiencing failure. One part of me needed to unlearn the false attitudes and ambitions that had grown over the years, but another side of me simply hurt for want of the reassurance of success and for want of the approval of old business friends.

It was around this time that I revisited the United States and was living with friends. As I looked around the city of New York I saw something different from what I had seen there before. I found myself identifying with the failures, the people that others didn't want to know. And it was on that visit that one evening in a state of some distress I first prayed. I was in my room and I simply asked God for wisdom and then I picked up a Bible and opened it and found I was reading the Book of Proverbs. I don't recall what it was I read but re-reading the text now there is much that must have been appropriate to me at that time.

Whom the Lord loveth he correcteth
Even as a father the son in whom he delighteth
Happy is the man that findeth wisdom
And the man that getteth understanding
For the merchandise of it is better than
The merchandise of silver

And the gain thereof than fine gold.
Wisdom is more precious than rubies
And all the things thou canst desire
Are not to be compared with her.

Back in England my material situation declined. I was still living well but I was living off capital, not off earnings. But perhaps my prayer was answered because I began to meet people and situations that helped me through this overwhelming sense of failure and self-doubt.

I remember meeting a young Catholic couple and though I wasn't converted to their faith I was strengthened by their sense of peace. I went to a spiritualist meeting and was told that a certain Swiss gentleman was speaking to me and was saying: 'Learn to know yourself'. At that moment it made no sense. The next morning it did, because slap in the middle of a shop window I saw a copy of *Memories, Dreams and Reflections* by the Swiss psychologist, Carl Jung. His own life story was one of a man who went his own way although the established world of psychology thought he had become a dreamer. He taught many things, but above all that we should trust our inner self – the self that emerges in dreams and in our interior promptings. Another helpful writer was the American philosopher, Emerson, who wrote: 'He has seen but half the universe who has not been shown the house of pain'.

I think that what I came to believe was that we have a soul, a spirit that is essentially at one with the creation around us and that in some way we are all of us messengers of the universe. We have responsibility to consciously live out this oneness by a way of life that cares for the planet and our fellow man and in the long run life itself will teach us this. My own ambition had been such that I had had to learn by failure, by finding that I simply couldn't be at home in a purely materialistic context. My nagging doubt had been my guide towards this belief. I spent some months in such reflections until the point when I realised that I could again take action, find some role that would both provide for my material needs and also my more spiritual motives.

I moved to Northamptonshire, a county criss-crossed by great modern communications network. The M1 motorway, the Grand Union Canal and the main railway to the north all pass within a mile or two of where I live. They seem symbolic to me not only of the tension between the material, technological world and the world of nature, but also of a kind of interconnecting function which I see as the role I can best fulfil. Now I run a hotel, not first to be a hotelier – though that itself teaches one to serve the needs of people – but to provide and organise a venue for weekend groups which meet to try to think their way through the crisis that our culture is undergoing, and to find ways in which they can help us all through that crisis. Participants come from all walks of business and the professions – both the establishment and more radical or alternative groups. All those who take part in those workshops have in one way or another experienced a crisis in their own lives. Like myself, they have all been brought to a point where they are searching for entirely new values. And I am myself still searching because the one question in my mind now is, in this time which is critical for all of us, how do I go about getting something done?

TRYING TO GO ON

During my short life in Ireland I learned a little of the beauty of the place. I also came into contact with the sorrow of the north. Then its sorrow became my sorrow. I lost what was closest to me, as so many there have done. Christopher and I were married for sixteen years. Perhaps not everyone would enjoy being a diplomat's wife but I loved it. I rather enjoy moving house – I always thought the next post would be the best of all. I make friends easily. I like organising things – whether it's a cocktail or dinner party, a children's Christmas party or do's for the embassy wives.

Our first overseas posting was to Algeria. There was still a savage war of independence going on and there was fighting in the streets of Algiers every day. I was, of course, worried for Christopher's safety. And when my second child, a son, was born it seemed as if something of the environment had rubbed off on him. He screamed night and day.

From the agony of Algeria we returned to a home posting. Domesticity took over. Kate was born safely within the protective walls of a London hospital. Then we went to Brussels – a very formal life. Cocktail parties, dinner parties. A very easy life surrounded by the affection of the anglophile Belgians. In 1971 we went to Paris where Christopher was Minister – the number two in the embassy – possibly the most sought after job in the Foreign Office. I adored it; I love the French; I love their huge capacity for communication; I love the challenge they present; I love the beauty of the city. We were there for four-and-a-half happy years.

News of our next posting arrived – Ambassador to Dublin.

But little did we realise that fate would no longer smile upon us. At the beginning of July we set off for Dublin and we went with great joy, hope and determination. Joy to be going to a beautiful country with a talented and articulate people; hope that we could contribute towards a solution to its problems; and determination that we would succeed. There had been a lot of publicity about Christopher beforehand. The first of his three novels had been banned in Ireland. There was one beach scene to which the Irish censor objected. It was indeed a coincidence to have a new British Ambassador who was both a writer and one whose work had been censored in Ireland. Christopher had a very clear idea of what he wanted to achieve there. I fully shared these beliefs, as indeed I did all his ideas.

Four days after we arrived he presented his credentials. It was a very formal affair, which impressed Kate, our youngest child, a great deal. In a little press conference he gave, the day before he was killed, to get to know the members of the Dublin Press Corps, he outlined the way he saw his mission there. He ended by saying, 'I see my role here as an exercise in clarification. I do not believe in the diplomacy of evasion. I very much do not believe in diplomats being cut off from the life of the country in which they live. My political philosophy belongs somewhere on the centre left . . . Things I saw in Algeria and in the second world war have given me one strong prejudice – a prejudice against violence.'

The day after, an act of violence, coming from a background of hatred and bitterness, destroyed him. He was on the way to the embassy and a landmine placed under the road, blew up his car, killing him and Judith Cook from the Northern Ireland Office and seriously injuring the other occupant and the driver.

My first thoughts were – I have lost my husband, the person I admired most in the world. I have lost the kindness, tolerance, humour and intelligence which he symbolised for me. Gone also is the work he intended to do for Ireland. Then I thought how dreadful if his assassination could impair relations between the British and Irish governments, the relations which he had so hoped to work towards strengthening. And then I thought perhaps at least I could salvage something. I could voice his hopes for Ireland and continue to work towards making his beliefs and ideals grow stronger.

There was a very moving memorial service for him set in the grandeur of St Patrick's Cathedral. I attended it with the children. Afterwards I invited many Irish people back to the embassy. I had to explain to them what Christopher wanted to do in Ireland. I had to tell them what an alive, wonderful person he was. I wanted to enlist their help in keeping his ideals and beliefs alive. In fact I stayed in Ireland for three weeks after his death in order to get the feel of the country and to meet some of the people he had hoped to meet and know.

The day of the memorial service in a short statement on Irish televison I said: 'I think many of you will have read that Christopher was a person who was particularly shocked by violence. None of us can afford to be equivocal about violence. Christopher was destroyed by it. But I am sure that Christopher's death will not be in vain and I hope it will make us more determined to work for these ideals which we share with him. I feel no bitterness, but I ask you to remember these convictions which he had and felt so passionately and which more than anything else I want to see bearing fruit'. The response from the Irish people was overwhelming. They wrote in their thousands. They wrote to tell me of their grief, their sorrow, their shame. And they expressed this with an eloquence, a passion that only the Irish can show. One person wrote – almost illegibly – 'You may be weeping your lost husband but we are weeping our lost honour'.

I felt if I worked towards turning the sense of loss and waste into something positive, trying to make at least something constructive come out of his destruction, then this might help and also it would help me not to feel any bitterness against the purposelessness and cruelty of the act. I explained to the children – who hate a public life – that if anything I did and they endured could save the life of one husband or daddy, then it was worth doing.

The memorial fund for Christopher was launched, with the support of many people not only in England, but in Ireland, France and Belgium. It is a memorial that has been made to fit with the kind of person he was – a fund to finance an annual literary prize. And the subjects are about the sort of things he believed in: peace and understanding in Ireland and closer co-operation between the countries of the European Community.

I became involved in the Ulster Women's Peace Movement. I first knew of it when I was on holiday with the children in France after leaving Dublin. I read an account in a provincial newspaper of one of their early peace rallies. It seemed like a glimmer of light at the end of the rather dark Irish tunnel. I wrote to them congratulating them on their courage and success and offering my help should they want it. When I got back to London I met the leaders of the movement. Betty Williams and Mairead Corigan are wonderful. They are both ordinary and extraordinary, they have a great gift of expression and their total sincerity is over-whelming. I feel very strongly that the influence of the women of Ulster on their children could contribute a great deal towards making the next generation of protestants and catholics live to-gether in harmony. My own children are an example of this for they have absolutely no feeling of bitterness towards Ireland. They think of it as a very pretty country where people showed them a warmth and kindness.

I felt I could help the peace movement with their 1976 London rally. They seemed to need people like me, uninvolved in politics, to stand for the English attitude. Perhaps I could represent an attitude of sympathy towards the problem of Northern Ireland and the wish of ordinary English people to see the violence and suffering there come to an end. I took part in the march and spoke at the meeting in Trafalgar Square. I tried to explain the aims of the Peace Movement as I saw them and the importance of our presence there that day. I said that regardless of their origin nobody was disqualified from caring about Ireland and sharing the convictions of the Peace Movement. I said, very passionately, that the hatred and violence of the few could not win, when faced with the courage and love of the many. I ended by asking the huge crowd to give the Peace Movement their support, their hope, their love. The rally, I thought, had an unqualified success. It seemed to generate goodwill and clearly had the overwhelming sympathy of all those who were participants or onlookers – the police, the taxi-drivers, everyone.

Now I am trying to patch a new life together for our children and for me. Henrietta and Kate are continuing with their education at the French Lycée in London and Robin has moved on to a new school. I have returned to work at the Savoy. Although the life, of course, is very different to being an Ambassador's wife, I am in fact working on the sort of things I know about from my old life. I am helping to decide about the décor of the hotels in the group and having quite a lot to do with the people who work in them. I feel I belong to something again. I was here when I first met Christopher so I feel I have moved round a full cycle. And life has started again – but less well because the person who mattered is missing now.

JACKY GILLOTT

A CRITICAL SHORTAGE

When I returned to live in the country-
side I wanted more than a pleasing view from the window. I
wanted a clearer view of how and why it was the great forward
rush of twentieth-century development had gone wrong. I
wanted to know at which points we'd been diverted on to tracks
with no real direction. I wanted to live somewhere where it was
still possible to see earlier patterns in the way a man worked and
in the way people lived together. I wanted to know if a closer
relationship to the land really did matter or whether it was
simply fanciful to imagine it did.

Well, by looking, I have learned considerably more about
the problems of farming. I know it can be more exhausting than
rewarding, that animals can be less reliable than machines; that
my beautiful view is somebody else's plain bread and butter;
and I've glimpsed both the good and the uncomfortable side of
closer communities. I have also learned – as W. H. Auden once
said – that the desires of the heart are as crooked as corkscrews. In
other words much of what I have discovered in my lovely hills
and valleys isn't what I thought I would find nor even what I
wanted to find.

The ironic discovery was this. Having spent some time writing
about a shortage in the industrial world's critical resources, I then
found I was short of basic resources myself – inner resources. I
don't think I'm alone in this deficiency. Poverty of spirit is, I
suspect, as much a product of the industrial age as the deep freeze
and the jump jet. There are thousands of us maybe who need not
fear smallpox or malnutrition, who have all the requisite arms,
legs, noses, whose pulse is regular and whose temperature is 98.4,

who nevertheless suffer from an indiscernible ailment. What is it exactly, this absent component?

In *Humboldt's Gift*, the writer Saul Bellow says that we have contrived a world which has no room in it for the spiritual sense. Those who adapt best are those with the least developed spiritual sense. Poets, men and women with an *acutely* developed spiritual sense, struggle like freakish throwbacks in this unholy place.

We forget that until we reached this small, rational speck in time's vast stream, men and women possessed souls and spirits and a God of their choice as naturally as they breathed air. And what are we to make of that? Were they all physically disturbed? Are all the people of this world who still regard it as perfectly normal to discuss the soul and the life of the spirit, are they all mad too? Well, not *all* perhaps but there are one or two. William Blake for instance. He was mad wasn't he? He actually believed rational thought was a refined means of destruction. He must have been mad. Was he? I'm not so sure any longer

In *The Marriage of Heaven and Hell* Blake describes a vision: 'I was in a printing house of hell and saw the method in which knowledge is transmitted from generation to generation. In the first chamber was a dragon-man clearing away the rubbish from the cave's mouth: within, a number of dragons were hollowing the cave. In the second chamber was a viper folding round the rock and the cave, and others adorning it with gold and silver and precious stones. In the third chamber was an eagle with wings and feathers of air: he caused the inside of the cave to be infinite; around were numbers of eagle-like men who built palaces in the immense cliffs. In the fourth chamber were lions of flaming fire, raging around and melting the metals into living fluids. In the fifth chamber were unam'd forms which cast metals into the expanse. There they were received by men who occupied the sixth chamber and took the forms of books and were arranged in libraries.'

What Blake feared – and what I've come to think he was right to fear – was the reductionist capacity of the rational mind, the capacity to distil the world's beauty into precise formulae.

He feared for a world that was being built on the narrow basis of science and logic. He thought that if we came to despise the apprehensions of the spirit, if we undervalued the resonant meaning of poetic symbols and overvalued the exactness of meaning contained within mathematical symbol, then far from building a society with a greater understanding of things, we would exclude the greater part of humankind from any sense of meaning at all.

Poetic symbols are democratic transmitters of meaning. They can be understood by everybody at whatever level they are ready to perceive. By poetic symbol I mean symbols that appear in religions and myths of every kind. The chalice for example, or the slain King, or the images that obsessed Michael Ayrton in his lifetime – the figure of Icarus, the Minotaur in his maze. These archetypal images appear in different forms in different cultures as if they signified coherent centres of meaning in human experience. They are part of our dreams as the quantum theory is not. Once they were part of our lives. But today when churches go unvisited, novels unread and storytelling is the factual business of televison news, a symbol is more likely to be a road sign or a manufacturer's trade mark than an emblem of human complexity. If we have favoured the rational rather than the spiritual, exact-itude rather than ambiguity, we may well have destroyed the kind of environment in which the spirit prospers. If we look at one another across the table, in the street, we look much as we have always looked. We don't look like a newly evolved species which has shed some unfunctioning part.

That is why we need artists, poets and painters who still possess a means of seeing, that expresses itself in images. If I try to see how a painter conceives of modern man, I quite often find that he has deserted the human form altogether or he presents a stylised form without a face, without features. There are painters who still present recognisable human beings. David Hockney for example. In his portraits of friends, he shows the gaze of those friends sliding past one another with a kind of blank alertness as though they don't really want to see one another at all. Or in

Andy Warhol's Marilyn Monroe series, the star's smile infinitely repeated by a machine process, the colouring of her features is deliberately over-printed so that other eyes sit alongside her eyes. That is a portrait of somebody being destroyed.

If I turn to another poet, W. B. Yeats, I find another disturbing image of man in *The Second Coming* – a poem that ends 'And what rough beast, its hour come at last. Slouches towards Bethlehem to be born'. This is how it begins:

Turning and turning in the widening gyre
The falcon cannot hear the falconer:
Things fall apart; the centre cannot hold:
Mere anarchy is loosed upon the world,
The blood-dimmed tide is loosed, and everywhere
The ceremony of innocence is drowned:
The best lack all conviction, while the worst
Are full of passionate intensity.

It is hard not to feel the force of prophecy in those lines and yet a few years ago that poem wouldn't have provoked the same powerful feeling in me as it does today.

I have to go back to the beginning to try and explain what happened – and I say try because, to be honest, I found it very difficult. I went to live in the country with a practical purpose. Everything I wanted to do I'd thought out up in the front of my head. I wanted to see how effectively one could, still, supply one's own needs because it seemed to me, if my premonitions about intensively industrial societies were in any way right, then all of us would have to learn again to work, quite literally, for our own living – for our food, clothing and so on.

Well, my efforts have been pathetic. Either I didn't know how to do things, or I wasn't much good at them even when I did know. Or I just let myself sink into compromise because in the end that was much simpler. But to go back to that poem of Yeats', I lacked – not conviction, but a confidence in my own conviction. My views seemed to have been forged by a typewriter rather than fire. Worse, I feared the fire, the passionate ntensity Yeats wrote about. Like him, I'd seen that fire in the faces of the crazy. So wariness made me resist a plucking response the landscape provoked in me. That was romantic. Indulgence. Any talk of the soul or the spirit I would have shrugged off then as nonsensical. I wasn't going to be sucked up by the trees, they were for wood, for burning. Animals couldn't beguile me. They were for eating. I wasn't going to be trawled through water. That was for washing.

But it was no good, everything I saw every day from the first gash of dawn across the dark to the last draining of light that left the orchards black against the sky, everything pulled and pulled at me until I was forced to take notice. So what was I fighting? Not the beauty of what I saw. That was undeniable. No, it was another factor, a kind of educated prudery, that tried to prevent the force of what I saw from seeping behind the eye and forming a colouration of the spirit.

I was so neatly tailored to fit the age in which I found myself that two learned responses blocked that transference. One was guilt. Guilt that I should enjoy what was, after all, a privileged view. And since it couldn't be widely shared, simply to look was self-indulgence. And to draw meaning from what I saw when others lacked the opportunity was downright offensive. The other blockage was academic, a wariness of the value of an emotional response in reaching an objective understanding of things. It was a nice paradox. I had come here because I believed a heavily rational bias had caused an ugly and dangerous tilt in our approach to things and yet my own conditioned regard for the supreme value of rational thought was so deeply entrenched, I was refusing to let the force of what I saw effect my thinking in any way. I was refusing, in exactly the same way as politicians and planners were refusing, to accept that our practical problems required anything other than practical solutions. I was failing to see that what we had weakened was not primarily our material resources, but our inner resources. Our means of perceiving. And that what we suffered essentially – what had brought us to our practical difficulties – *was* a spiritual crisis. And that it was here, in our way of looking at things, in our attitudes and values, that changes most needed to be made.

I didn't care much for this conclusion. It sounded feeble. It also sounded reactionary. I was dismayed to find myself occupying the same platform as people whose moral zeal had always been grotesquely unattractive. But finally it seemed to me, that if the problem was one of spiritual crisis, then I had to have the courage to allow what I'd come to accept was some form of spiritual response in me – even if it was a little more than paganism – to flow freely.

The idea of this surrender was quite terrifying. For all I knew, this was the catastrophe of the insane mind. I feared – I still do fear – the intensity of spiritual experience. To lay one's mind open to the force of what is invisibly apprehended is not a very serene activity. But to be open, to respect the spiritual instinct has meant that it no longer seems affectedly mystical to me to climb the hill behind my house each evening and go to look down across the wide, flat plain, once sheeted by water, to the distant point where Glastonbury Tor rises. It doesn't seem absurd to look at the old Celtic field shapes, mere shadows on the hillsides now, and feel time slide by into an unbroken continuum. I'm not ashamed of attaching significance to what I see – deny it and one risks a life full of insignificance. What I've learned from looking at the changes of light, the beasts, the seasonal alteration of crops and colours is to praise, yes, but also, to have an altered sense of proportion.

In today's terms my freedom to live in the countryside is a privilege, but only in today's terms. For the greater part of human history man has lived in a close relationship with his surroundings and that couldn't help but affect his view of things. Knowing that, I see that it isn't fanciful to seek through it a unity of body and mind and spirit, but on the contrary, such unity is evident in all natural forms. Only man who has denatured himself, built his own, unnatural citadel, strikes away from it. And I can see that inevitability, not immorality, has led to God's eviction from the city where all evidence of form is man-made.

In a world where shelter, transport, fabric have been fashioned by human genius, inevitability, not stupidity, has led men literally to lose sight of the earth which truly sustains them. Not deliberately, but inevitably, man has become God. He is the maker of things, he is the healer. He is the law-maker.

But to see what you eat either grazing or growing in a field, to rely on something as wanton as weather for your physical labour to be fruitful, to know that a bitter frost can be a good and necessary thing, to handle animals who respond to your care by giving of themselves, to witness constantly, that death is the precursor of new life, not merely the end of an old, is to be made ceaselessly aware of one's relatedness. You are part of the whole, steward rather than sovereign. And the humility this engenders isn't a cowed and feeble thing, but a means of understanding I think John Donne was striving to express in his Twelfth Holy Sonnet:

Why are we by all creatures waited on?
Why do the prodigal elements supply
Life and food to me, being more pure than I,
Simple, and farther from corruption?
Why brook'st thou, ignorant horse, subjection?
Why dost thou bull and boar so seelily
Dissemble weakness, and by one man's stroke die,
Whose whole kind you might swallow and feed upon?
Weaker I am, woe is me, and worse than you,
You have not sinn'd, nor need be timorous.
But wonder at a greater wonder, for to us
created nature doth these things subdue,
But their Creator, whom sin, nor nature tied,
For us, his creatures, and his foes, hath died.

Even in Donne's London, 350 years ago, the creatures of the countryside presented an apparent contradiction which he was able, as poet and churchman, to resolve in a meaningful way. In a similar way, the countryside and its creatures have helped me. It's not that the beauty of nature demonstrates the existence of

God, but it does help explain why belief has become so difficult for urban men and women.

I don't think God resides solely in the countryside. Nor do I see God in every tree – if I did I'd feel obliged to dance round them, and I don't. But I think I've come to feel closer to the Cornish poet, Charles Causley, when he writes:

God who does not dwell on high
In the wide unwinking sky
And whose quiet counsel starts
Simply from the human heart
Teach us strong and teach us true
What to say and what to do
That we love as best we can
All thy creatures, even man.

SHEILA HOCKEN
FIRST SIGHT

Until last year my world was a totally
different place. I had been virtually blind since birth. I could see
light and dark, and colours. But I suppose it was like looking
through a really thick fog. And last year I had a successful operation to remove a cataract and I found myself in a totally new
world.

When I was growing up, I was ashamed of being blind. I
would never use a white stick; I would never ask for help. I
would try and live normally and mix with people. But it made
me feel imperfect. I would go out in the evening with friends,
perhaps to a dance, but it was always so embarrassing. Something
would always let me down. When you can't see it's so difficult to
cover things up. I would sit there and hope somebody would
come and ask me to dance. And then when I thought they were
going to, I would hope that they wouldn't because I wouldn't
know what to do about it. It got to the stage when I was a teen-
ager that I was afraid to go out in the evenings.

I remember asking my mum if she knew when she had
children that blindness was hereditary. She said she did, and I
was horrified. To me in those days everything was black or
white. I asked her why she had a child knowing it could be
blind. She asked me if I'd enjoyed my trip out with my friends
the other night. And, of course, I said I had. 'Have you enjoyed
your life generally?' she said. Well yes I had. 'Well that's your
answer. Do you want life taking away from you?' That made me
realise that I'd got a really full life to live and I wanted to live it.

It wasn't until I got Emma, my guide dog, that I became more
self-confident. It was marvellous to have Emma, she gave me

complete freedom as far as mobility was concerned. And that meant I was able to make a lot more friends and I was able to go to many different places. I went horse-riding, I went to evening classes where I learnt to sew on an electric sewing machine. That was very hair-raising and very frustrating. I remember one evening trying to put a zip on a dress and I tried sixteen times before I actually succeeded. I also gave talks to sighted people about guide dogs. It wasn't that I particularly wanted to do any of these things, but I just had to prove to other people that I was as good as they were. I would have hated to have anybody say: 'Oh poor soul, she can't do it because she can't see'.

I did eventually have all the really good things in life though. I had a really good job as a telephonist, I'd got Emma and I had a marvellous husband, Don. I met Don on a blind date after talking to him on the telephone. I couldn't see, he could but that didn't make any difference because we really felt that we understood each other.

It was the little things that were so frustrating – like letters. I would hear them land on the mat in the morning, I could pick them up, I could feel them, I could smell them, but I still couldn't read them. I would go to the cupboard for food, pick a packet out and then discover I'd forgotten how to mix it. I would know the instructions were printed on the back but I just couldn't read them. And when I got a tin out of the cupboard I'd just hope it was green beans and not rice pudding that we were going to eat. Or I'd walk along the pavement and bump into a wall that I thought was a person and ask when the next bus was due. That was most embarrassing and frustrating.

I had always wanted to see, of course, if only to be able to see to read and to be able to see where I was going and what people looked like. But if somebody had asked me: 'Don't you want to see flowers or grass or trees?' I suppose I would have said 'yes' but how can you really want to see something you've never seen before?

I had seen a lot of specialists when I was a child and growing up but they'd all given me the same answer: there wasn't much they could do. Then we heard of a specialist who was using new techniques. Maybe he could do something now, so I made an appointment.

It was a cold, January day, and sitting on the bus on the way to see the specialist I thought of all the things that I wanted to do when I could see. I sat in the waiting room hoping and longing, that this was going to be the day, this specialist was going to be able to do something this time. I went in to see him. He had a look at my eyes and he sat back and 'ummed' and 'Ahhed' a bit and I said: 'Well can't you do anything?' He said: 'Not really, I might be able to try'. That felt like somebody had burst my bubble. I wanted to get hold of him by the lapels and shake him and say: 'You've got to do something'. But I said: 'Well couldn't you try, I've got nothing to loose?' He said: 'Well I might be able to give you a bit of sight'. I asked him if the operation was successful would I be able to read?' I remember him telling me then that he didn't work miracles and no, he couldn't give me that much sight. I felt very disappointed but having nothing to lose I decided to go ahead with the operation.

I had to wait nine terrible months for the operation. All I wanted to do was to talk about what it would be like to see. Everybody else wanted to play it down and not really discuss it, especially my husband. I think he was worried about me building up my hopes in case it wasn't a success.

I had the operation on a Friday and I had to wait until Monday before they took the bandages off. On the Monday morning I sat in the ward, waiting for somebody to shout me to the dressing room. And when the word came, mentally I was down the ward at fifty miles an hour, but physically I was still sat there. I was so scared. When the bandages came off and I saw light for the first time, it was like an electric shock. The first thing I saw was the white of the nurse's apron and it was so brilliant that I had to turn away. And there were blues and greens, shades and colours that I never knew existed. I knew what blue and green were, but they weren't at all like I remembered them. They were brilliant, beautiful colours. The bandages were only taken off for two minutes that day and when I went back down the ward I was in a world of darkness again. But oh, what a different place it was because I could now remember all those colours I longed to tear the bandages off and rush to the window and see what the world was like outside.

It seemed an absolute age before they took the bandages off altogether and I was going home. When I came out of the hospital it was like the first sunshine, like the first day. It had never been there before, how could it have been, I'd never seen it. And I had this notion inside that somebody had made it just for me, just for that very day. When I saw grass for the first time I just couldn't believe it was so green. I had to kneel down and touch it to make sure it really felt like grass. There were trees everywhere, so many different shapes. I never imagined trees grew like that, they were beautiful.

It was autumn when I came out of hospital, a time of year I had always loved. A blind person can smell autumn and when you feel the leaves underneath your feet, its so beautiful. People had tried to describe to me how leaves changed from green to gold, red and brown but when I saw it for myself I couldn't believe the host of different colours. I had to pick the leaves up and take them home with me. Surely, it was all a dream.

I found animals were perfect too and also beautifully coloured. Lots of people had tried to describe Emma to me. They had told me that she was a chocolate-coloured labrador. I saw her first in the sunshine when I came out of hospital. She had a ginger nose and ginger ears and her back went to ebony and russet, and so many different shades of brown that I just couldn't find the words to describe them.

Every morning when I get up now, it's so exciting, for there are so many new things to discover. I like to go out and watch the traffic and the people go by, or I just sit and look at our living room. The fireplace, for instance, is fascinating. There are so many different colours to the bricks, different shades, different textures. Blues and beiges and beautiful colours. And how could you ever describe to a blind person what woodgrain looks like.

It is so beautiful I could lose myself in pools of woodgrain.

At first my brain took a long time to unscramble visual images, everything I saw I had to touch to know what it was. The first meal I ate was a salad. I thought it would be so easy to eat when you could see, but it wasn't. I would aim for a piece of tomato and miss. When I went to the shops for the first time, I didn't know where they were so I had to put Emma's harness on and ask her to take me. When we got out on the pavement I looked down and with horror I saw the pavement moving beneath me. I saw the posts and the hedges wizzing past. It was terrifying. It was silly really but just one of the things I had to get used to. When I used to go out with Emma people were so helpful. They would give me a seat on a bus, open doors for me, traffic would stop. But now, nobody seems to take any notice.

Just before Christmas, I had a baby, a little girl. I still don't know yet whether she will be able to see or not but she seems observant, alert and very watchful. If she can't see, there are lots of things I will be able to help her with, to tell her. But if she can see, it will be marvellous. We will be able to discover things together. I shall be able to share her world more than any other mother in the world.

WILLIAM ALLCHIN
TO SHAKE HANDS
ON THE RIVER KWAI

This is a story about bridge building. First, I helped build one of the many bridges that carried the Japanese railway along the edge of the River Kwai. It was for the enemy, to help transport the Japanese army on its way to Burma in the second world war. Then, later, I learnt the Japanese language in an effort to bridge over another kind of division, that of nationality and language and the experience of being enemies. Then with psychotherapy, I tried to help bridge over the splits in the personality, to work for some real healing of the mind, my own and those of others.

Men seem inevitably divided, not just split in themselves, but split by nation, language, by even religion. So much of it is bitterness from the past. This was further underlined for me when I re-visited the River Kwai and came to believe there was still a bridge to be built – one of reconciliation.

In 1942 I was a soldier on a troopship, the Empress of Asia, approaching Singapore. She was attacked by Japanese bombers. The ship was hit and set on fire. I remember feeling intense fear coupled with curiosity. I found myself looking around and actually wondering what happened when bombs hit ships. In fact, I remember it getting very hot and we went down on ropes into the sea and had to be picked up. We came in on the last ten days of the disastrous Malayan campaign. There was confusion and demoralisation. Key personnel were being evacuated which added to the hopelessness of those left behind. Some men deserted and tried to reach the docks. When we capitulated we had, in fact, more men on Singapore Island than had the Japanese. No wonder they despised us, especially us officers, who had been part of one of the most serious defeats in the long history of the British army.

I imagined from my schoolboy knowledge of history that we should have tried to fight to the last man and the last round. When the white flags went up it was quiet and I felt a mixture of relief, shame and apprehension. The next day we marched across the island which was cluttered with the debris of war and defeat, abandoned equipment, corpses, shattered vehicles, to be concentrated into the first of our camps around Changi.

Well, that was the start of it all. At first the camps were reasonably well regulated, hours of work were not unlimited, and although food was short, it was fairly shared out. Smaller camps away from the central areas were more hazardous. Then, early in 1943, parties started going to Thailand. The belief was that conditions of life were better there and I was disappointed not to leave Singapore for Thailand until May of that year.

The journey up to Thailand in railway cattle trucks was grim. It was a suitable introduction. Our destinations were camps in the jungle and immediately we got there, we started work. We worked long hours, under pressure, sometimes leaving the camp before daylight and returning in the dark. Poor rations, injuries, fatigue, added to the gradually increasing list of illness, such as malaria, dysentery, malnutrition, vitamin deficiency, and later cholera. The pressure went right down the line and we were at the end of the pecking order, along with the Asian workers. The Japanese and Korean soldiers reacted to pressure too. People were shouted at, hit, sometimes knocked down and kicked. Others were punished by being made to stand in the sun holding a big rock over their heads. I never myself saw anyone killed on these occasions but sick men had to go out to work and death came in many and various ways.

Eventually I found myself working at one of the camps near to the Burma border in the last drive to get the railway finished. I don't know if I was different from others but I don't think so. I rate my experience of working on the death railway as about average. Some of the Japanese were Christians, some were

Buddhists, Shintoists or whatever. At all events they certainly weren't all sadists. I remember once I was going out to work with legs swollen by beri-beri, and ulcers caused by infected wounds from the sharp bamboo undergrowth. On this occasion, a Korean guard saw me and taking me to the British camp HQ he said that I must have four days in camp. It was a surprising and embarrassing incident but I was relieved to have the extra rest. At another time, working on a high bridge, a Japanese army carpenter saved me from falling off when I over-balanced, in an attempt to wield a heavy hammer.

But the casualty rate was very high. In October 1943 the railway was completed and trains began to run. It was exciting to see a locomotive in the jungle. The pressure eased a little, and many of us were taken back to Singapore and it was there that I first heard the gospel preached and the enemy prayed for. When I heard this man preach the Sermon on the Mount it had a compelling power for me and though I was brought up in the church, I felt a Christian in a new way. 'You have heard the saying, "An eye for an eye and a tooth for a tooth". But I tell you, you are not to resist injury. Whoever strikes you on the right cheek, turn the other to him as well. Whoever forces you to go one mile, go two miles with him. You have heard the saying "You must love your neighbour and hate your enemy". But I tell you, love your enemies and pray for those who persecute you. Then you may be sons of your father in Heaven. You must be perfect as your heavenly father is perfect.'

Later on I began to learn Japanese and started to give English lessons to a Korean soldier. I could count up to thirty in Japanese and deal with simple routine matters. If anything went seriously wrong or the guards got very angry, then I could not understand enough and the situation could quickly get out of hand. But none of the people I knew were interrogated or tortured, though many died of disease.

On my return to England I made a three-day retreat with the Cowley Fathers in London and finally decided to study medicine. My army and POW experience had made a great change in me.

For a start my class attitude had been uprooted. In the army I first encountered working-class England. In Malaya and Thailand I worked like a labourer myself. Many English men had lorded it over Asians in those places. We were the first who had to take the reversal of roles. It was a salutary experience and profound in its political and symbolic importance. Hitherto it was the white man who supervised, who gave orders, who was free. Now the Japanese were giving the orders. I believe that much of the anti-Japanese feeling stems from this although few English people really understand it even now.

I continued to try to understand the war and what it had meant. I saw exhibitions of pictures in London of Auschwitz, Belsen and Buchenwald concentration camps in Nazi Germany. I realised that the Japanese perpetrated nothing like that thought-out systematic, cold-blooded genocide. Some cruelty, some indifference, some ruthlessness, yes. But not extermination of personality or persons as happened in those camps in the heart of Europe.

Eventually I found my way into psychiatry and began to draw together some of the fragments of my own life and personality. But the Sermon on the Mount and work of reconciliation seemed to remain as a continuous theme, an inescapable commitment. I keep around me as I work in my consulting room, reminders of the work of others who have lived by the same commitment. 'Be merciful as your Father is merciful. Also judge not and you will not be judged yourselves. Condemn not and you will not be condemned, pardon and you will be pardoned yourselves, give and you will have ample measure given you. They will pour into your lap measure pressed down, shaken together, and running over for the measure you deal out to others will be dealt back to yourselves.'

It came about that I returned to Thailand early in 1976. The opportunity simply arose and I was happy to take it. I was taken by surprise to find that most of the forty people who travelled out from England with me, former POWs with wives and friends and others, soon showed that they still felt deep bitterness and hostility to the Japanese. We went to the railway where we had worked and I was surprised to find that this was now the end of the line. But deeper feelings seemed to be centred around the graves, in the cemeteries of Kanchanaburi and Chunkai which we visited. I was caught by an idea that any of these men buried there might be entitled to interrogate me, to ask what I had done with my thirty extra years, to justify my good fortune.

As a survivor of the camp, I believed and still feel myself to be under an obligation to work for peace and reconciliation. I believe that the people who died would be more likely to endorse this view, than the maintenance of a continuing bitterness. But I know that many people feel it to be disloyal to those who died to have any contact with the Japanese. But however you look at it the Christian gospel is quite specific on the points of peace-making, reconciliation and justice.

It was a Japanese, Mr Nagase Takashi, who first put forward the idea of a special get-together on the river Kwai to mark the 33rd anniversary of the completion of the railway. As soon as I heard of the idea I knew it was right that a genuine move from Japan should be met with a genuine response from us. But in the end we couldn't make up a party from Britain to go out to the Kwai Bridge to meet others from Hong Kong, Australia and Japan. It was then that we hit on the idea of having a supporting meeting in London. The obvious is often overlooked. A trip to Thailand is expensive. All of us who were out there are now older, some already on pensions, some have jobs and commitments with little chance of saving up for such a trip. And the time in which to organise it was limited. So the meeting in London took shape. Bishop Appleton suggested the Jerusalem Chamber at Westminster Abbey with all its rich and tragic associations. We made our witness there on 25 October almost totally ignored by the British press, but reported and filmed for people in Japan to see on television.

I have touched on the shocks which started to make me a more conscious and aware person. After a quiet and orderly upbringing my effort of discovery had to be made into the area of chaos.

Hence the war was the shock and the POW camps, the university. In my background, anger was controlled, inhibited, repressed. In war-time violence pays and gets confused with heroism. If animals are in conflict it is often enough for one of them to make a threat, a noise, to indicate opposition for the other to get the message and desist, or go off elsewhere. But man is not content, he must overpower, humiliate, destroy. He insists on unconditional surrender. For him, in his imagination, the final solution is elimination of his enemy from the face of the earth. So violence produces violence. Hurt avenged, vengeance revenged. Our task is to see how to cut through these 'archaic cycles' of violence and revenge.

As Jesus said, 'They who take the sword shall perish by the sword'. There is no final solution in that sense. I believe that the man we kill becomes part of us. We take his life and share his death, and set all his friends, relatives and colleagues against us. Someone has to make the first move, to take the risk to say no more of it, as Jesus put it, to begin to take away the sins of the world.

In the camps I learned to be glad that I hadn't had to kill anyone in the war. We learned to cooperate. When the heat's on, men want to go every man for himself and not risk working together. And yet our only hope is to learn to share, to communicate, to work together. As a tourist, returning to Thailand, an affluent westerner among poor Asians, there was a continuing sense of unease. That was to feel one form of violence. To feel the old antagonism of those who continue to see the Japanese as the enemy was to be challenged again to find the way forward. As the Welsh poet, Waldo Williams wrote:

Forgiveness is finding the
way through the thorns
to the side of the old enemy.

BIOGRAPHICAL NOTES

Anne Bancroft was born in 1923 and was brought up in the Quaker village of Jordans in Buckinghamshire. She married first at seventeen and then again at twenty-five and is the mother of four children. After some years in America with her second husband she and her children returned to England and she trained as a teacher. She subsequently became a Lecturer in Comparative Religion. Now married again, she is the author of *Religions of the East* (1974) and *Twentieth Century Mystics and Sages* (1976).

Maeve Binchy was born in Dublin, where she went to a convent school and then took a degree in history at University College. She taught in a girl's school in Dublin until 1968 when she joined *The Irish Times* as Woman Editor. Five years later she was appointed London Features Editor of *The Irish Times*. Her first play *End of Term* was performed in Dublin's Abbey Theatre and her book of collected articles from *The Irish Times* was published last year.

Lionel Blue was born in the East End of London, and was educated at Baliol College, Oxford, and at the Leo Baeck College, London. He is a Rabbi, and now teaches at the Leo Baeck College, and is Convenor of the religious Court of the Reform Synagogues of Great Britain. He has written *To Heaven with Scribes and Pharisees*, and *A Taste of Heaven* with June Rose. He is also co-editor of *Forms of Prayer* and is vice-chairman of the Standing Conference of Jews, Christians and Muslems in Europe.

Jack Burton was born in 1939 and educated at the City of Norwich School. He trained for the Methodist ministry at Handsworth College, Birmingham, and served as a minister in Glasgow and Ely. Since 1968 he has worked as a Norwich bus-driver. He has written two books, *Message Delivered* (pseudonymously, 1967) and *Transport of Delight* (1976).

Sheila Cassidy was born in Lincolnshire in 1937. She studied medicine at Oxford University where she obtained a degree in Physiology. Her clinical training was at Radcliffe Infirmary and she qualified as a doctor in 1963. Her book *Audactiy to Believe* was published in 1977.

Colin Cowdrey was born in India in 1932 and educated at Tonbridge School and Brasenose College, Oxford. For some twenty-five years he played first-class cricket, captain of Kent for fifteen of them. His publications include *Cricket Today*, *Time for Reflection*, *Tackle Cricket This Way*, *The Incomparable Game* and last year his autobiography *MCC: the autobiography of a cricketer*.

Bill Edwards, 51, was educated at Bedford School, Christ Church, Oxford, and the Harvard Law School. He was called to the Bar in 1952 and taught law at universities in Britain and Canada. After two years in Wall Street as a lawyer, he returned to Britain. His activities since his return in 1957 have included: Director of International Nickel Ltd; legal practice; Chairman of Rent Assessment Committees, Rent Tribunals and National Insurance Tribunals.

Jane Ewart-Biggs had a conventional British education followed by various jobs. These included working in the Foreign Office and the House of Commons before she married her diplomat husband in 1960. She now lives in Chelsea with her three children, and works for the Savoy Group as advisor on the décor for the hotels. She has also been deeply involved with working for Ireland through the Northern Ireland Peace Movement.

Jacky Gillott was born in 1939 and educated principally at a grammar school in Lancashire. She studied English at University College, London, and went on to Sheffield to start an ill-advised career as a newspaper reporter. In 1963 she joined the BBC's Radio Newsreel and since then has broadcast on a number of arts and current affairs programmes. Her books include *Salvage* (1968), *War Baby* (1971), *A True Romance* (1975) and *Crying Out Loud* (1976). She is married, has two sons and lives in Somerset.

Vera von der Heydt was born and educated in Berlin. She came to live in London in 1933. She trained in analytical psychology with Dr John Layard, in Oxford, Dr C. G. Jung and Dr Jolande Jacobi in Zurich and Dr Gerhard in London. She is a professional member of the Society of Analytical Psychology; training analyst, Association of Jungian Analysts; and Honorary Fellow, the Guild of Pastoral Psychology. She now practises as a Jungian analyst in London, is a frequent lecturer and broadcaster and author of *Prospects for the Soul* (1975).

Archie Hill was born in the West Midlands in 1926. He has worked as an iron moulder, a glass blower and was six years in the RAF where he became an alcoholic. He spent two years in prison and struck rock bottom when he landed up as a meths drinker under the arches. His autobiography *Case of Shadows* was published in 1973. Since then he has written fifteen radio plays, twenty-eight morning stories for radio and six books, including *Corridor of Mirrors* (1975), *Summers End* (1976) and *Closed World of Love* (1976).

Sheila Hocken was born in Nottingham in 1946 and was educated at a secondary modern school. She was registered blind but managed to get through ordinary school with help from teachers. She became a telephonist when she was nineteen and at the age of twenty-nine had an eye operation which enabled her to see properly for the first time.

Satish Kumar was born in 1939, received no formal education and became a Jain monk at the age of nine. At the age of eighteen he joined Vinoba Bhave in his Land Gift Movement. He was Director of the London School of Non-Violence and has written *Non-Violence or Non-Existence* published by Christian Action. He has also written a book *Journey through the World without a Penny* in Hindi. He is editor of *Resurgence* magazine and his autobiography, *No Destination,* due to be published in December 1977

Bel Mooney was born in Liverpool in 1946. Her family moved to Wiltshire when she was 14 and she was educated at girls' grammar schools. Whilst reading English at University College, London, she met and married Jonathan Dimbleby, and they now have one son, Daniel Richard, age 4. After university she taught briefly, then worked on the staff of *Nova* magazine. Since then she has freelanced for a variety of newspapers and magazines. At the moment she is European Editor of the American magazine *Viva*, and is writing her first novel.

Erin Pizzey was born in China in 1939. She is the founder of Chiswick Women's Aid and her book, *Scream Quietly or the Neighbours Will Hear*, was published in 1974.

Cicely Saunders was born in 1918 and educated at Roedean School and St Anne's College, Oxford. She trained as a nurse at St Thomas's Hospital. She later became a medical social worker and finally studied medicine in order to work with the problems of pain in terminal illness. She founded St Christopher's Hospice which opened in 1967. She was awarded an Honorary Doctorate of Science at Yale University, USA, in 1969 and a Lambeth Doctorate of Medicine in 1977.

Robert Van de Weyer was born in 1950 and educated at Westminster School and Lancaster University. He lived in India for two years after leaving school, working as a teacher and then for the Village Industries Commission. In 1973 he went to Ethiopia to explore its monasteries. In 1975 he published *Guru Jesus* about his conversion to Christianity. He now works as an economist, lecturing in Cambridge, and is currently writing a book on the relevance of theological and moral thought on economic life. He is married with two sons.

John Wyatt was born in Ashton-under-Lyne and educated at the town's technical school. He started working life as a 'copy boy' at the Manchester office of the *Daily Telegraph*, but enthusiasm for the countryside led him to a post of forest worker, since when he has been a subpostmaster, camp site warden, and an organiser for Oxfam. He has been Head Warden of the Lake District National Park since 1960. He regularly contributes articles and short stories to papers and periodicals. He has written several books, best known being an autobiography, *The Shining Levels* (1973).

Paul Yates was born in Belfast in 1954. Poet/painter, he has held several exhibitions of his visual works, examples of which are housed in private and public collections both in Great Britain and abroad. Two collections of his poetry have been published to date: *A White Cat with a Human Face* and *Sky made of Stone*. His play *Heap* was first performed at the Queens Festival, Belfast, and later at the Institute of Contemporary Arts, London. His third collection of poetry is shortly to be published and he is at present working on his first novel.